I'M SO GLAD YOU GLAD YOU TOLD ME

What I Didn't Wanna Hear

BARBARA JOHNSON

I'M SO GLAD YOU GLAD YOU TOLD ME

What I Didn't Wanna Hear

WORD PUBLISHING

Dallas·London·Vancouver·Melbourne

PUBLISHED BY WORD PUBLISHING, Dallas, Texas

ISBN 0-8499-3654-3

Printed in the United States of America

For almost twenty years, a sparkling, dark-eyed beauty
has been the pivoting factor in bringing great joy
and true delight to our lives.

For that reason,
I am thrilled to dedicate this book to her:
Shannon, my darling daughter-in-love.

Shannon and Barney Johnson with daughters Tiffany, left, and Kandee.

Contents

Acknowledgments

*I*f this book provides a comforting word, a bright spot in your day, it is because of the many people who have graciously shared their words and feelings in these pages. Because they want to reach out to other hurting parents, more than one hundred of them granted me permission to share portions of their letters written to Spatula Ministries.

Names and details have been changed to protect identities, but the situations they describe and the feelings they express are very real. When you read their letters, I hope you'll realize you're not alone in your pain. I also hope you'll find, in their encouragement, the strength to hang on, even if it's moment by moment.

To lighten things up, a host of talented writers and artists have also agreed to lend their wit, words, illustrations, and cartoons to give you a boost of humor to hammer out your pain. I'm grateful to them for being willing to share their gifts.

Diligent effort has been made to track down the source of the jokes, poems, cartoons, and stress busters included in these pages; if you find an error in the attributions, please notify the publisher in writing so corrections can be made in future printings.

Special thanks to Ashleigh Brilliant of Brilliant Enterprises, 117 W. Valerio St., Santa Barbara, California 93101, for letting me adapt his Pot-shot #2313 for the title of the book and also for the other clever Pot-shots that are sprinkled throughout the book.

Additional special thanks go to:

John McPherson for allowing me to include four of his wonderfully zany cartoons in Chapters 3 and 8.

Suzy Spafford of Suzy's Zoo for letting four of her delightful little creatures visit these pages.

Argus Communications for allowing me to use the words from one of their posters as the title of Chapter 1 and also for letting me adapt the poster as an illustration in that chapter.

My friend Charlene Baumbich and her publisher, Servant Publications, for sharing, in Chapter 2, an anecdote out of her book, *Mama Said There'd Be Days Like This But She Never Said Just How Many.*

To Rich Cook Jr. for letting me include in Chapter 9 some of the lyrics to his joyous song, "Buried Alive."

To RGA Publishing Group, Inc., for allowing me to reprint motivational anecdotes from the books *Psyching Out Diabetes* and *Diabetes Type II and What to Do.*

To Marilyn Goss and Arts Uniq' for sharing, in Chapter 7, Marilyn's beautiful depiction of Psalm 91:11.

To Roy Mathison for sharing his "Smile Awhile" cartoon in Chapter 7.

To Vicki Rush of the *Pryor (Okla.) Herald* for sharing the wisdom of "Mr. Hooty" in Chapters 3 and 8.

To the King Features Syndicate for allowing me to use Wayne Stayskal's "Ralph" cartoon in Chapter 9.

To Jeremy Iggers and Longmeadow Press for sharing the silly "Answers Price List" from *Off the Office Wall.*

To Jeffrey Cummings of Bethany Farms, Inc., St. Charles, Missouri, for letting me reprint the poem, "'Twas the Night before Jesus Came" in Chapter 6.

To the nice folks at Recycled Paper Greetings for letting me use, in Chapters 5 and 8, the ideas expressed in two of their clever greeting cards.

To Robert D. Smith of First Image, Inc., for sharing, in Chapter 8, "Fifty Famous Parental Sayings" by comedian Andy Andrews, author of the best-selling book *Storms of Perfection.*

To Dr. John Cocker and Stoddart Publishing Co., Ltd. for the "strings of your heart" cartoon in Chapter 5.

To Tribune Media Services for letting me use the "Buckets" and "Mother Goose and Grimm" cartoons in Chapter 8.

To United Media Syndicate for the "Peanuts" cartoon included in Chapter 5.

To Universal Press Syndicate for the "Calvin and Hobbes" cartoon in Chapter 7 and to Ziggy and Friends, Inc. for the three "Ziggy" cartoons in Chapters 2, 7, and 9.

To Shirley Boozer for sharing the encouraging words of her great-grandmother, the late Pearl Waddell, in the poem, "I Wish My Friends Could Only Know" in Chapter 7.

To Anthony Westling and Portal Publications for portions of the greeting card titled "All I Need to Know about Life I Learned from My Support Group" reprinted in Chapter 7.

I'm also pleased to include in chapter 7 a little poem that is reprinted by permission of the publishers and trustees of Amherst College from *The Poems of Emily Dickinson*, Thomas H. Johnson, ed., Cambridge, Mass.: The Belknap Press of Harvard University Press, copyright © 1951, 1955, 1979, 1983 by the president and fellows of Harvard College.

Helen Lowrie Marshall's poem, "Answered Prayer," in chapter 6 is used by permission of Warren S. Marshall, manager, Marshall Enterprises, Littleton, Colorado.

The silly questions to the "Action" column reprinted in chapter 5 are used with permission of the *St. Petersburg (Fla.) Times*.

Now you are sad, but I will see you again and you will be happy, and no one will take away your joy.

John 16:22 NCV

The Truth Will Set You Free . . .
But First It Will Make You Miserable*

*Of all the things I've lost,
it's my mind I miss the most.*

*M*others seem to have a sixth sense about impending disasters. It's as if we have a built-in radar system attached to an invisible satellite dish that constantly whirls on top of our heads, anxiously searching for any hint of trouble. Otherwise why would the classic warnings come so easily to us?

"You'll put your eye out with that thing!"

"You'll be sorry!"

"You'd better take a sandwich. You're gonna get hungry."

"Slow down!"

"Hurry up!"

"You have no idea what you're getting in to!"

Because we have this built-in early-warning system, mothers—and dads, too, for that matter—often sense when bad news—*really* bad news—is about to be dumped on our doorstep. One dad wrote:

> When our son said he was coming home to see us
> and to talk about his future plans, I sensed my most

---

* The title of this chapter and the accompanying cartoon on page 5 are adapted from a poster published by Argus Communications, Allen, Texas 75002, © 1976. Used by permission.

closely held fears, my concerns about his sexuality and his current roommate who had been his constant companion for the last three years. . . .

The evening after he arrived home I had to attend a church meeting, and I returned home after my wife was in bed. When I got into bed, she began crying uncontrollably. I knew. I just knew. . . .

When the bad news we've been dreading finally comes, we find ourselves caught in a terrible dilemma: On one hand, we want to know the truth—and on the other, well, sometimes we'd rather have surgery without anesthetic than hear the devastating news about to be dumped on us:

"Mom and Dad, I'm gay."

"I have AIDS."

"I'm on drugs."

"I'm so sorry, Mr. and Mrs. Smith, your son . . . I'm *so* sorry—"

Reeling in shock, knocked senseless by pain, yet somehow relieved that we've survived what we've sensed was coming, we stagger backward and ironically think, *I'm so glad you told me what I didn't wanna hear!*

At least the waiting is over. Now we can progress, unencumbered, toward full-fledged panic, that point we've always anticipated as we've told ourselves . . .

> One day I shall burst my buds of calm
> and blossom into full hysteria.

Those of us who've heard heart-breaking pronouncements can't help but laugh now at the things that *used* to send us into orbit:

"Like my hair, Mom? It's 'Napalm green.'"

"I'm getting an F in English."

"I dented the fender."

"I lost your credit card."

"I burned the cake and destroyed the kitchen, but the rest of the house is still standing."

"I'm moving out."

"I'm moving back home."

INSTRUCTIONS:
As bad news approaches,
flash this sign.

Earning Our Credentials

As bad as they were at the time, those formerly disastrous announcements seem pretty tame to us now. Of course, we're different people than we were then. That was back when our lives seemed peaceful and our families were normal.

Now we're thankful if we can manage to have even one moment of peace, and we haven't felt normal for a long, long time. Instead, we are ready for admission to the Home for the Bewildered.

Dear Barbara,

Lately I have had several fears that I may be going off my rocker. How can I know if this is what is happening to me?

               Fearful in Fayetteville

Dear Fearful,

We know that one out of every four people in this country is mentally unbalanced. So, you just think of your three closest friends. . . . If they seem to be okay, then you're the one!

We've been through the wringer.

We've walked through the fire (that aroma we wear is the smoky scent of lingering disaster).

We've crawled our way through the tunnel (some of us are still groping through the darkness).

But in the trials we've faced, something good has happened too: God has fine-tuned us so we are more compassionate, more caring, more loving, more aware of others' pain. When I speak to groups around the country, I always like to introduce

**The
truth
will
set you free,
but first
it will
make you
miserable.**

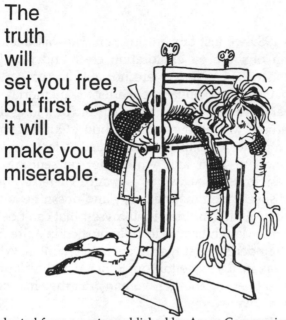

Adapted from a poster published by Argus Communications,
Allen, Texas 75002, © 1976. Used by permission.

myself as one who has "CREDENTIALS FOR SHARING"—not
just as some lady up there being funny and cracking jokes. I
have been through the valley, I have wallowed in the pain, and
I've been where lots of folks are now. I know by the mail I get
that a lot of other parents out there have these credentials too:

> In September 1994 we received a letter from our
> son stating that he is gay. The heartbreak we felt can
> only be understood by others who have been there
> and are walking this same path.
>
> Only three years earlier we watched our young
> daughter die of cancer. I thought then that nothing
> could hurt as bad. But I have learned that we have
> different pains that hurt beyond description. We
> have peace knowing that our daughter is with Jesus
> and will never hurt again. But our gay son—what
> happens to him?

❦ ❦ ❦

In 1989 we lost our darling son. He was working for an offshore oil exploration crew and was lost overboard. . . . They were not able to recover his body. Our other son left here after the memorial service and we haven't seen him since. For a long time he refused to talk to us on the phone. Our last word was a postcard stating he had quit his job and was moving out west and would not be sending his address to us. That was a year ago. There has been some speculation that he is gay and doesn't want us to know. As his mother, I tell myself that can't be! In 1991, our daughter was terribly burned in a fire. She is still undergoing surgeries every six months. While she was in the hospital, our other daughter's husband left her for another woman after they had been married twenty years. . . .

Warning: Laughter Ahead!

Considering the pain that surrounds us "credentialed" parents, you should know we've cried a river of tears over the crises we've faced. But if you're a newcomer to this elite group, you might be surprised at what you'll hear (or, I should say, *read*) in these pages.

We're gonna have a good time.

We're gonna laugh.

Yes, *YOU* will laugh!

I know what you're thinking: *You got the wrong number, sister. Maybe those other folks can find something to laugh about, but you haven't heard* MY *story yet. It'll snow in August before I can laugh again!*

You think no one else has a problem as bad as yours.

You think you're the only one who has lain awake at night wracked with the stomach-churning pain you're suffering. You think no one else has felt like an elephant was sitting on her chest. You can't believe anyone has ever had an invisible shag rug stuck in his throat. Maybe you even think you're the only person whose teeth itched!

And, above all, you probably feel like you're all alone in this trial.

You're wrong.

All of us hurting parents have wrestled with that elephant, and even now I sometimes feel that shag rug creeping back up into my throat. My teeth haven't itched for a long time— but I'll never forget how it felt when they did! The important thing is to KEEP BREATHING . . . and KEEP BELIEVING! There is hope for all of us hurting parents, no matter how deeply mired in the mud we are.

**Today is the tomorrow you worried about
yesterday—but not nearly enough.**

Part of my purpose in writing this book is to help you learn to live with heartache when happy endings are not in sight and when long-term anxieties seem to hang on indefinitely. One of the ways I'll do that is to share the "testimonies" of other parents who have heard bad news—and survived. And to help ease the stress you're feeling as you fight your way through the cesspool, I'll share some of my favorite stress busters at the end of each chapter and in assorted "peelings from the ceiling" sprinkled through the pages to keep things from getting too serious. These little ditties are things I have found or heard during my travels around the country, or they've been sent to me by the many people who've learned, as I have, that laughter helps flatten out the pain. They made *me* laugh. I hope these frolics of foolishness give you a chuckle too.

Dear Barbara,
   My teenage kids will not accept our rules, and they are giving me continual fits. What can I do?
                                        Fitful in Philadelphia

Dear Fitful,
   The smartest advice on raising kids is to enjoy them while they are still on your side. If it was going to be easy to raise kids, it never would have started with something called LABOR!
   One mother of three notoriously unruly youngsters was asked whether she would have children if she had it to do over again, and she replied, "Yes, but NOT THE SAME ONES!"

The reason most people change their minds so often is that they never find one worth keeping.[1]

You know the only people who are *always* sure about the proper way to raise children? Those who've never had any.[2]

I need some of my problems
to help take my mind off some of the others.
                          Ashleigh Brilliant
                          Pot-shot #551 © 1974

Another title destined to be a bestseller:
Kids Are from Mars.
Parents Are from Cleveland.[3]

When Jesus said, "In this world you will have
trouble," He wasn't kidding! (See John 16:33.)

This is a test.
It is only a test.
If this were your actual life,
You would be given better instructions.[4]

A little girl and boy walked hand-in-hand to a
neighbor's house. The girl was barely able to reach
the doorbell. When the lady, a family friend,
answered the door, the little girl said, "We're Mr.
and Mrs. Jones, and we're playing house. May my
husband and I come in?"

Deciding to play along, the woman invited the
couple in and offered them lemonade and cookies,
which they happily accepted. But when a second
tall glass of lemonade was offered, the little girl
refused.

"No, thank you," she said. "We have to go now.
Mr. Jones just wet his pants."

Mental floss regularly with God's Word
to avoid truth decay.[5]

Sign painted on house destroyed by earthquake:
"The fat lady has sung."[6]

Dear Barbara,
  My doctor insists that I must begin a vigorous
exercise program. Can you suggest one?
                    Plump in Petoskey

Dear Plump,
  The most important thing to remember about
exercise is to start SLOWLY . . . and then taper
off. And remember this: The easiest way to get a
healthy body is to MARRY one!
  There is one exercise that I tried, and it
SOUNDED so simple . . . I was supposed to
bend over my vacuum cleaner and extend my
right leg behind me while I touched my head to
my knee. This was just before my vacuum sucked
up my nightgown and caused me to completely
pass out!

I had to give up jogging for my health . . .
My thighs kept rubbing together and setting my
pantyhose on fire!

WARNING!
HUMOR MAY BE HAZARDOUS TO YOUR
DEPRESSION.[7]

A little boy's prayer:
   Dear God, take care of the whole world. And
please, God, take care of Yourself, or we're all
sunk!

Blessed are they who clip coupons,
      for they shall be redeemed.[8]

When I die, I want to die peacefully, like my
grandfather did, in his sleep . . . not screaming,
like the passengers in his car!

WOMEN: Remember, as we get older we are no longer having hot flashes. They are now called power surges![9]

For God has not given us a spirit of fear, but of power and of love and of a sound mind.[10]

2

I've Learned to Accept Birth and Death, But Sometimes I Worry about What Lies Between!*

*I used to be lost in the shuffle.
Now I just shuffle along with the lost.*

One of the most comforting things for hurting parents is discovering there are *hundreds* of other parents out there who have gone through the same painful struggles—and survived. That's the main idea behind this book—helping to comfort parents in pain by sharing the stories of *other* parents who are out there on the dance floor of life, doing the "lost-parent shuffle." As one woman wrote,

> Please, Barbara, continue to share the letters of those suffering pain because of alienation with their children. No two letters are the same, but each letter speaks to me just when I need the support. And please continue showing us how to laugh during this tribulation. Your humor has carried me through more than one black period of pain.

Other mothers wrote:

---

* Ashleigh Brilliant Pot-Shot #92 © 1968.

13

You help comfort us hurting moms . . . because you have been through the "fire" and we can all feel it! Please write another book with lots of letters from people—such comfort!

       ⑥ ⑥ ⑥

I can't begin to tell you how much it helps knowing you are not going crazy and there are other people facing the same problems you are and getting through them. Life can be painful, but I believe praying for and building coping skills is the key.

I always believe that we find out who we are in the gray and black times in our lives. Life is such a great gift, and I want to be very much in it, even though at times when I hear news that causes my heart to drop to my stomach I wish I could just quit and scream—ENOUGH!

Like Jesus, I want to say, "Please lift this cup from me." It is a constant struggle, but I do feel myself growing, and for that I am thankful.

A Gift of Love from Your Fellow Pit-Dwellers

This book is meant as a gift of love to you from your fellow strugglers down here in the pit. But never forget that you have Someone who is far better than all the "credentialed" parents in the world: You have Jesus! He promised us, "I am with you always."[1] And remember what the psalmist proclaimed: "The good man does not escape all troubles—he has them too. But the Lord helps him in each and every one."[2]

Jesus knows what it's like to suffer; He suffered on our behalf! And He also knows what it's like, late at night, to feel such heartache you think you'll die. On the night before He was crucified, He led His disciples to Gethsemane and told them, "My soul is overwhelmed with sorrow to the point of death."[3] And certainly He knows what it's like to feel all

Two are better than one . . . For if
they fail, one will scrape the other off
the ceiling. *(Eccles. 4:9–10, adapted)*

alone, because those same disciples—His closest friends and
followers—suddenly disappeared when the bad times started.

Jesus knows how you feel—hurt, scared, alone—and He's
always with you to wrap you in His comfort blanket of love.
But maybe right now you're in such a state of shock that you
can't accept that promise.

Maybe you're like the little boy who was afraid of the dark
and wanted his mother to stay in the room with him at bed-
time.

"Son, I can't see why you're so afraid of the dark. Don't you
know God is with you?" the mother asked.

"Yes, I know that," the boy replied, "but I want someone
with skin on."[4]

If you need "someone with skin on" right now, this book is intended just for you. I've got lots of skin—too much, judging by my looks. But I always remember this important rule of life:

**You're not old
unless you get wrinkles in your HEART!**

My heart has been wrung out so many times it's bound to be wrinkled, but I am continually rejuvenated by the laughter I find all around me. I hope to share some of that joy with *you* in the pages of this book, but one of the most important things for you to understand is that I'm not writing this book alone. It's a compilation of some of the *thousands* of letters I've received from parents just like you and me—parents in pain. Parents who've landed on the ceiling and need someone to lovingly scrape them off with a spatula of love and set them on the road to recovery.

One woman who landed on the ceiling wrote to me the day after she'd learned that her son was gay. In her state of shock, she wasn't even sure she could write the word "homosexual." She said, "Barbara, I can't even spell—is that a clear sign of my condition? And I can't have my secretary type this—it's too personal!

Learning to Laugh Again

Freshly shocked parents usually believe they will never recover from the trauma, and they certainly don't ever expect to laugh again. But gradually, they learn to see humor all around them. One woman helped her friend learn to laugh again by giving her a copy of one of my books, *Mama, Get the Hammer, There's a Fly on Papa's Head.*

> She read it . . . in the car as she and her husband drove back and forth to work. . . . She laughed so hard her husband asked her, "Are you sure this book came from a *Christian* bookstore?"

A lot of the parents who write to me haven't reached this point yet. They're still stuck on the ceiling . . . groping through the tunnel . . . smoldering in the fire. Although it's painful to read their letters, I want to share them to let you know you're not alone in your anguish. You may even discover there are other parents who have come through worse things than you. Most of all, I hope you'll see there are many parents who have been as devastated as you are—and they're still breathing. And, as incredible as it seems, many of them *have* learned to laugh again.

> At a time when my husband and I were having some financial troubles, I was feeling awfully sorry for myself when I started reading your books. Not only did they make me laugh, they made me *extremely grateful* for all that I do have. I'm slowly but surely learning to give all my troubles to the Lord and letting go for good.

Another wrote . . .

> I can't believe how much your books have helped me realize there are actually people going through worse times with their children than me. And there are people who actually have the same feelings that I have. . . . The sudden loss of an adult child for no apparent reason is really hard. You have so many expectations for them, and then they turn away from everyone who loves them and you don't know if they are dead or alive— that's hard!

The Trials of Jobella

I'm not sure why it's curative to hear that other people are enduring more severe problems, and I certainly don't claim to have any healing properties myself. But I've been through a lot of heartache over the last twenty years. And I'm not out of the cesspool yet. In fact, when one woman heard about my ongoing struggles, she wrote:

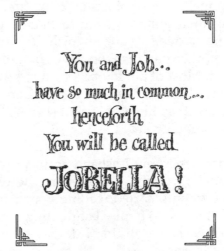

You and Job... have so much in common... henceforth You will be called JOBELLA!

I love this nickname because it reminds me of all that poor old Job went through—and still he was steadfast in his faith, knowing he would survive. He said, "Though He slay me, yet will I trust Him." Job knew his troubles would end someday. Then, he knew, God would "fill [his] mouth with laughter and [his] lips with shouts of joy."[5]

Like Job, I know my problems won't last forever. To remind myself of this, I frequently quote that wonderful King James phrase that reminds me my trouble didn't come to STAY. Again and again in that beautiful old version, the words appear: "It came to PASS."

Of course, there ARE exceptions to this "came-to-pass" rule, especially the mysterious staying power of a phenomenon that occurs in chocolate shops:

HOW IS IT THAT YOU CAN GAIN TWO POUNDS BY EATING HALF A POUND OF FUDGE?[6]

Just when my husband, "Gopher" Bill, and I think things are as bad as they could possibly be—when we've finally made it to safe harbor—another hurricane comes along. That's when the shag rug starts creeping up into my throat again. One letter-writer put it well when she said,

> Help! We need a giant spatula! My husband says he feels like one of those moving ducks in a penny arcade. We just pop up, thinking blissfully that the worst is over . . . and bang! we get shot down again.

This Too Shall Pass

Enduring Faith—and Wacky Foolishness

The two things that got me through all the agonies I've faced were a tattered but enduring faith in God and a wacky sense of humor. I've shared what I've learned in my books, and as a result I've learned a lot more from parents whose letters pour into my mailbox (more than a bushel of letters a day!).

While some letters are cries of anguish from parents who've just landed on the ceiling, many others are from those who've finally made it to the shore of life's cesspool. Now they're finding warmth in the sunlight of God's love, they're laughing again, and best of all, they're eager to throw a lifeline to others who are still swirling through the sludge. They know:

**TO LOVE AND BE LOVED
IS TO FEEL THE SUN FROM BOTH SIDES.**

Here's what some of these parents said:

> Barbara, I know I'll make it. *We* will make it. Then maybe I'll be able to help someone else.

> ❦ ❦ ❦

> Since our world was turned upside down by the news from our daughter that she is a lesbian, God has done so much healing—beginning a month later when He miraculously put your *Geranium* book in my hands. His healing has continued and as I've read so many times from other parents, He has changed my heart and given me a capacity for love that is miraculous!

> ❦ ❦ ❦

> After reading the two letters from the mom whose son just announced he was homosexual, I had goose bumps. My husband and I, having gone through the same thing ourselves, perfectly understood her fears for tomorrow. I would like to share this thought with her:
> Never stop trusting. Never stop hoping. God is faithful and will answer your prayers in due time. Yes, the road will be hard, and the tunnel may be long, but never forget that you are not alone in that tunnel!

Thousands have been experiencing what is now new to you. We feel for you and will pray for you, that through this you will have a deeper understanding of who God is. Never forget that HE is going through this dark tunnel with you and that He will shed His marvelous light of encouragement along the way. That will make all the difference in the world.

When you hurt, He hurts. He promised to never leave or forsake you, and His promises are trustworthy.

It has now been five years since our son announced the same news as yours did. . . . I was so shocked, I cried all night. . . . I kept repeating, "not my son, not my son," as if that was going to change anything. . . .

This is the time not to lean on your own understanding, but on the wisdom and compassion of our wonderful God and father.

While most parents who write to me are mothers, one of the most hope-filled letters came from a father who wrote the following letter several years ago. When I asked this man for permission to share the letter here, he said he and his wife reread the words he wrote so long ago. "Amazingly," he added, "they still ring true." His letter is long, I know, but I hope you'll read every word of it because its message offers hope and down-to-earth suggestions for parents who have just landed on the ceiling:

It has been close to two years now since our college-age son told us he was gay. Guess what, Barb? We're still here! Even more, we're smiling and praising God. No, our son hasn't "gone straight," but we are experiencing God's peace. God has been so gracious to us in so many ways through the ministry of Spatula that we feel compelled to share where we've been and where we are; hopefully, it will offer some encouragement to others who will travel our road.

My wife and I plummeted through the same range of emotions you experienced and described in your book, . . . shock, disbelief, "this must be some mistake," "we can fix it," and hope. Yes, I suppose that is the word that best describes where we are now: HOPE. Not hope that he'll change but hope that grows from a confidence in what we've always experienced in our lives when we thought we knew what was best for us . . . the knowledge that God has a better idea.

This letter is not so much a story about our son as it is a story about his parents and how we "survived." There were a number of aspects to our survival, no single one standing on its own, no magic cure-all.

Though there was no pill we took that made it better, surely Spatula was at the center of our road to wellness. Not just Spatula on its own but the insights we gained by immersing ourselves in the love of those who shared and understood our hurt. This gave us an opportunity to pour our hearts out in a non-threatening, non-judgmental atmosphere, without fear of criticism. Also, we received the assurance from others that we *would* survive!

Another brick on the path to recovery was when we got past our introspection and attended to reaching out to others who were hurting. We give thanks because God gave us an experience that allowed us to empathize with the deep hurts of others. As we began reaching out to those who were hurting we began to cope with our own pain . . . and eventually our pain began to subside.

It is important to have someone you can trust your innermost feelings to, someone you can share with, apart from your support group. We were blessed in that many of our immediate relatives were comforting and understanding of our situation, so we didn't have to live a secret life. Undoubtedly that played a major role in the rate of our recovery. Not to suggest that everyone was comfortable with the issue of homosexuality, though a vital few were. What a blessing!

The next big milestone came when we stopped focusing on straightening out our child and acknowledged that that was God's role. He fixes 'em. We love 'em. An aspect of that was being able to accept our child for who he was and where he was, moving away from a position that assumed he was the way he was by some considered choice of his own. This is not to say we exulted in his circumstances; rather, we reminded ourselves that God loved us unconditionally and that He would have that be a model of our love toward our children.

This was a major factor in the restoration of our relationship to him. When he recognized that we were not preoccupied with straightening him out, he was able to let down his defenses and freely express his love toward us. Also it allowed him to freely share his hurts and fears with us. (It's funny how our stereotypes imagine a person totally given to sexual expression. The reality is that the fears and hurts of the homosexual are generally those that we ourselves experience. I believe the burden of their homosexuality does, however, heighten their pain in relationship to what others might experience.)

Another insight came to us as we weighed the advice of the well-meaning that we should distance ourselves from our child; that insight was the importance of a healthy parent-child relationship in the restoration of the child and the parent (yes, *both* need to be restored!). Never does a child need the love and security of his parents more than when in the throes of dealing with his or her homosexuality. Even a casual knowledge of the homosexual issue shows the vulnerability of the homosexual to the drug scene and suicide. What a terrible time to abandon your child, right at the time when he needs you most!

How can I wrap up this long-winded letter? We still hurt, but less often than not. We are still afraid, but rarely. We are not naive. We know there will be pain down the road. But the good news is that God is in control (wasn't He always?). We have a deeper, more loving relationship with our child than before. We have new friends that we never had before, friends who love us with the full knowledge of our circumstances. We know the fulfillment that comes from reaching out to others with empathy and helping them get through a tough time. We look forward with anticipation to what God's plan is in our lives . . . and ahead to how He will take this low point in our lives and turn it to more blessing. We've moved from "Why me, Lord?" to "Thank You, Lord!"

The Price of Loving

As you read the letters in this book, remember that these writers are people "with skin on." They're real people. Living, breathing souls who know what it's like to be tormented by the actions of—or loss of—someone they love. As one woman wrote,

> Sometimes I wonder why it can hurt so much. I guess it is the price for loving. "Love anything and your heart will be wrung and possibly broken"— the line from C. S. Lewis is so true.

Frankly, I prefer a more optimistic "lesson" I saw recently in one of those little "rule books":

> Gather all the crumbs life throws your way. Soon
> you'll have a lovely, thick slice of memories.[7]

Almost all of the letters I receive come with legible signatures and return addresses—from all over the world! Whenever I could track down the letter-writers, I've asked for and received permission to use the letters appearing in this book. The only changes are some slight editing when needed and the altering of details in letters to protect the identities of sons, daughters, sisters, brothers, spouses, or friends.

The emotions you'll read in these letters are powerful. There's a lot of pain here, but there's humor too. One mother of a homosexual wrote,

> Yesterday was the pits—I felt forgotten, abandoned,
> cheated, and my health is so filled with pills that it
> is a wonder I can still crave a hot fudge sundae!

Another friend sent "one little joke for your cheering section":

> You've heard of the twelve-step program, but
> have you ever heard of the ONE-step program?
> "WHAM! Get over it!"

These letter-writers share my love for the promise in Proverb 11:25, that as we refresh others we, ourselves, are refreshed. This is what I like to call BOOMERANG REFRESHMENT.

With this in mind, I want to remind you again that we're gonna have a good time in this book. Trust me. But first I want you to meet some more of the folks who are plastered onto the ceiling with you so you'll understand that you're not alone in the feelings you're experiencing.

One of the first obstacles parents feel when the bad news comes is a combination of ISOLATION and SHOCK. If that's what's happening to you, I hope you'll read these letters and know you're not alone:

One of the hardest things to deal with when this happens is the isolation you feel. The secrecy and the shame are so constrictive, so restrictive, so lonely. . . .

A Russian "brother" . . . often told of a prison-camp torture. It is called the "cement sack." It is a cement cubicle only big enough for a person to stand in for solitary confinement. In my feeling of isolation with this pain, and the feeling of "no way out," I could relate. . . .

⑤ ⑤ ⑤

Our daughter left college and joined a cult. I nearly lost my mind! . . . She left the cult after two years but immediately informed us she was a lesbian. The last few years have been a living nightmare. . . . I cannot talk about this with anyone. . . .

⑤ ⑤ ⑤

We have survived the longest and most difficult day of our lives and are exhausted with the effort. . . . Our son apparently has been dealing with the issue of his homosexuality for over a year and decided this is the way he is. We were able to remain fairly calm, to reassure him of our unconditional love. . . . He said, "I'm not going to start wearing dresses, march in parades, or any of that. I'm the same person you have always known . . . except now you know more about me."

He told us to prepare for a period of grieving. He's already endured his. We all agreed that it was both extremely difficult and extremely trusting for him to come to us and tell us of this part of his life. We shared tears, hugs, and a few laughs. We parted as friends.

But now we begin our journey through the tunnel . . . and it looks like it will be a long one.

© © ©

I learned four months ago that my daughter is gay. As you well know it hit me like a bomb. I do know what it is to have a broken heart. I enjoyed your book and it helped to know what another mother goes through. I did not hide in my bedroom and count the roses on the wallpaper as you did, but I did and still do cry. . . . I will never stop praying for my daughter, and I know that God can do all things. . . . I think as mothers we want to fix things, and we know we can't fix this.

These letters remind me of that little axiom that says:

The secret of dealing successfully with a child . . . is NOT to be his parent!

The Badge of Heartache

When parents describe their feelings of shock and isolation, I'm reminded of how devastated I was several years ago when our son told us that he was homosexual "or maybe bisexual." I was so ignorant in those days I didn't even know what "bisexual" was. I thought it might mean having sex twice a month—and in my befuddled state I wondered why on earth he would tell me THAT!

Back then I didn't know anyone who had a homosexual child. Now, because of our ministry, I hardly know anyone who doesn't! After my son told me he was homosexual, I frantically looked for another MOTHER to talk to—a mother who could tell me how to cope with the impossible. Recently a woman whose twin sons died of AIDS described the mother-to-mother connection this way:

It is strange that when you hurt so badly and it
eats into every fiber of your body you become deaf
and dumb. I say dumb because the mind does not
function. Grief for your child is something that only
a mother who loves her child can understand.

ZIGGY By Tom Wilson

ZIGGY © 1995 ZIGGY AND FRIENDS, INC.
Distributed by UNIVERSAL PRESS SYNDICATE.

Another woman reached out in prayer to another mother
she had never even met but knew must be hurting too:

> Always I bombard the throne of God to keep my
> son safe from harm and to turn him from his destruc-
> tive lifestyle. My prayer never changes. I always
> pray for my son's "friend" also because I know he
> has a mother whose heart is breaking just like mine.
>   I am still in the closet because I can't bring myself
> to tell anyone. . . .

When I first learned my son was a homosexual, I couldn't

find another mother who had gone through the pain I was experiencing. Remembering those feelings of panic, I can easily sympathize now with the parents who write to us at Spatula Ministries, crying for help. They want to know that SOMEONE out there cares about them. Many of them describe the scars of their pain as matching the treads of a steel-belted radial:

> We have discovered the reason our daughter and her husband are getting a divorce. She is a lesbian— or maybe a bisexual, she says. This is an Oh-My-God experience, as Chuck Swindoll says. I asked her twice if she was sure, but deep down I knew. It hit me a week ago, and I have been trying to bury it by saying, "Oh no, it's all your imagination." I think God was preparing me for this shock. But I am not prepared enough. Could anyone ever be prepared for this news?
>
> I have been hit by a truck. I lie face down on the pavement. Slowly I raise my head. Every bone in my body hurts; my head throbs and my joints still feel the weight of the dual wheels. I am aware of every nerve in my body, the tingling in my cheeks, my dry mouth that feels like it is stuffed with a giant ball of cotton, my knotted stomach.
>
> "What more could happen?" I think. Deciding I have lain there long enough, I raise my head slightly, slowly, placing my palms on the pavement and drawing my knees toward me in an effort to get up. "You have to get up," I say to myself. "You have to go on."
>
> Then the driver of the truck sees me from a distance.
>
> He puts the truck in reverse, racing the engine. He backs over me again.
>
> That's the way I feel. . . . I wonder what else could happen. I idly think, "Oh, I suppose my husband could have another heart attack and die."

The next day he calls me at work. He is having chest pains. . . .

As I drive to the hospital I think about the day nearly twenty years ago when our son died. I stood in our back yard, tears streaming down my cheeks, shaking my fist at God, saying, "Why me?"

And the answer came, softly, quietly, "Trust Me."

Yesterday I lost my diamond from my engagement ring I had received thirty-one years ago. My calendar for that day said, "There is nothing that cannot happen today." When I saw it, I burst out laughing. Losing the diamond would normally be very upsetting to me, but it is really insignificant at this time. I still have the wedding ring. I still have my husband and daughters. . . .

෦ ෦ ෦

We learned this week that our son has declared himself to be a homosexual. . . . We are both numb and devastated. . . . His birth was, literally, an answer to prayer. He has been a committed Christian and never even had a traffic ticket, never smoked nor drank alcohol. . . .

Now we find ourselves beginning a journey we don't want to take. We see our son making choices that can only hurt him.

We are lost. . . .

A lot of other parents feel lost too. They could leave behind a notelike the on the next page.[8]

Bolts of Lightning

While many parents have a hint of foreboding when bad news is about to be dumped on them, for others it's a bolt out of the blue. I've received a lot of late-night "911" calls from these desperate parents. One distraught mother called me from an airplane. Her son and his girlfriend had driven her to

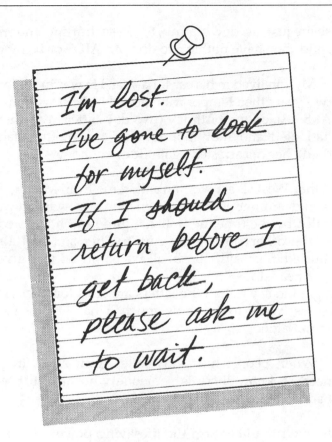

the airport, and as she got out of the car, she said to her son, "I'm so glad you have such a nice girlfriend."

Her son turned to her and said, "Mom, it's time I told you. She's not my girlfriend. She's into girls, and I'm into guys." And with that he set her bags on the sidewalk, gave her a hug, and drove off! I'm not sure how she knew to call me, but she did—from thirty-five thousand feet! I sent her some of my books and materials. A few days later she called back and said she had shown the material to her boss and he had asked her to "repeat the order" for someone in his family who has a gay child.

Not all of the parents who need help are struggling with issues of homosexuality. Believe it or not, there are problems that seem just as devastating to these hurting moms and dads, and they have nothing to do with AIDS or being gay:

> My son lived in his car for a year. He was in jail for two years then temporarily moved back in with me. At 5 A.M. on my birthday (two days after my father had died and four months after my mother had died), he was arrested again from my home. . . .

Another West Coast woman called me from Miami, where police had summoned her when her son was murdered. Tragically, by the time the police figured out how to contact her on the other side of the country, her son had already been buried. She said, "Barb, all we could do was give him a proper headstone."

I'm glad to say not all the letters are cries for help. A lot of people just write to say how much it has helped to learn they're not alone:

> When people hurt, no matter from what, they need to know there is someone who has hurt as badly as they do and survived.

Others write to confirm the lifesaving power of humor in times of crisis. As one mother said:

> **We laugh to survive.**

This letter-writer has also learned the truth of Carol Burnett's statement:

> **Humor is tragedy plus time.**[9]

Other parents have written to say how much they need ongoing encouragement from those who truly understand what they're enduring:

Our wonderful church friends are loving and supportive, and they continually pray for us and with us concerning our sons. . . . However, they do not understand the depth of our pain the way a parent who has been there could ever understand. Therefore our need for encouragement from your ministry.

⑥ ⑥ ⑥

Thank you for sharing with me. . . . Wouldn't it be nice to get up just one day without thinking about it??!! It helps to know someone is walking the same path. If you can survive, maybe I can too!

P.S. You know what's hardest sometimes? Letting go of the beautiful dreams we had for our precious sons!

⑥ ⑥ ⑥

I would still be wallowing in self-pity, but thanks to the encouragement of your books and hearing other parents share their journeys (of course we thought we were alone!), we can count ourselves survivors. There are still tears, and my heart aches for my son, as you well know, but I have given him and this whole matter to God, and it is because of the tools you have given me that our family will be able to enjoy a merry Christmas this year.

⑥ ⑥ ⑥

There are many times you feel you are the only one that has family problems or went through tragic deaths of family members. After reading some of the letters from other people, you realize you are not the only one.

⑥ ⑥ ⑥

I guess part of what helped me was to realize that there are a lot of people who have worse or more severe hurts than I do, including you, Barbara, and if you can smile and get through it, so can I. I've been miserable for ten months and it's time to get on with life. . . . Thank you for making me smile again and for letting me see that life does go on.

⑥ ⑥ ⑥

There are so many blessings that have resulted in my husband's confession to me of his devastating financial misdealings. When we went to bed that first night, we were both exhausted. However, I could not sleep. I was compelled to get up out of bed and get a Bible. The pages fell open to Ecclesiastes 3—"There is a time for everything." . . . I devoured every word of that passage and was overwhelmingly filled with such hope and felt God's grace engulf me. . . .

There was anger, hurt, questions (that never got answered), bewilderment, etc., ad nauseum. I knew I had a mission. Sell the house, get a handle on our finances, keep the kids on a positive note, maintain our unity, continue carpooling, volunteering, and all of the other daily activities that we take for granted when a crisis is not on the horizon.

Barbara, I don't know how I would have started on that positive road without my dear friends sending me your *Geranium* book. I remember lying prostrate on the kitchen floor of our million-dollar home and praying to the Lord to "give me the strength that Barbara Johnson has." I vowed that if you could get through what you had gotten through, I could get through this.

⑥ ⑥ ⑥

To know that the phases I have gone through (and return to)—the crying, the withdrawing, the rebelling, the praying, the questioning, the reading, the bewilderment, the self-condemnation, and on and on—are "normal" has helped me survive.

ⓦ ⓦ ⓦ

At times I have felt abandoned by our friends in the ministry. Your books have helped me overcome some of the hard times. I am more than willing to let you have that herd of elephants back from off my chest—and you can have the shag rug back too. I am still searching for my sanity, and the song that the scarecrow sings in the *Wizard of Oz* has become my theme: "If I Only Had a Brain."

ⓦ ⓦ ⓦ

With God's help and through the help of Christian friends and family we made it through our dark tunnel.

How thankful I am for such letters, letting me know families are surviving the agony that's plunged them into the pit. I'm also thankful to those friends who, knowing how much I love funny stories, write to share humorous tidbits, silly jokes, and embarrassing moments with me.

When I told my friend Charlene Ann Baumbich I was writing a book about parents receiving bad news, she shared this funny "bad-news" anecdote from her book, *Mama Said There'd Be Days Like This, But She Never Said Just How Many:*

George and I were engaged in lively conversation when he stopped talking for a moment and retrieved his white no-frills hanky out of his back pocket. Unfolding it, he vigorously blew his nose. I continued to talk without skipping a beat.

After several good snorts, he folded the hanky right on the creases, again and again, until it was returned to its perfect square. He put it in his right hand and slid it down into his back pocket.

When he looked up at me, I had become mute. My mouth was agape. I couldn't believe what I was seeing, and it showed on my face.

"Is something wrong?"

"Do you *always* fold your hanky like that after you blow your nose"

"Yes. Is that a problem?"

"Maybe."

"Why?"

"After twenty-five years of married life I had no idea you folded your hanky back up like that after blowing your nose."

"So?"

"So, I'm sorry to tell you that when I'm doing laundry and find the hanky so neatly folded in your back pocket, I assume it hasn't been used and I simply put it back in your drawer without washing it."

Now it was George's turn to stand with his mouth agape. After a couple of beats passed, he responded, "No wonder I always have so much trouble getting my glasses clean."[10]

George and his smeared glasses remind me of a letter that said:

> Sometimes our days feel like a smudge on the window panes of life and we don't dare look out of them for fear of what we might see.

It was these "smudges" of life that prompted me to pack a windshield wiper in the bag of "props" I take along when I'm speaking to groups around the country. I use it as a reminder that if we let Him, God "windshield wipes" away our worries. He polishes off our smudges of pain, rubs off any mistakes we've made (or think we've made), and gives us a bright, new outlook on life. Then, instead of focusing on the "oughtas" and "shouldas" and "if onlys," we can fill our minds with thoughts that are good, pure, and lovely as God renews us from within.[11]

To have this kind of attitude we need a *different* kind of glasses, the spectacles my friend Roger Shouse calls "Grandma's glasses." He tells the story of a little boy who said to his friend, "Wouldn't you *hate* to wear glasses?"

"No," his friend replied, "not if I could have the kind my grandma wears! My mothers says she can always see when folks are tired or discouraged or sad. She sees when somebody is in need, and she can always recognize when you have something on your mind that you need to talk over. But best of all, she can always see something *good* in everybody!"

The little fellow continued, "I asked my grandma one day how it was that she could see that way. She said it was because of the way she's learned to look at things since she's gotten older. So I'm sure it must be those glasses of hers!"[12]

Wouldn't it be wonderful if all of us could see others through Grandma's glasses?

God's Waiting Room

Just as Grandma could see something good in any situation, God can take your trouble and change it into treasure. Your sorrow can become joy—not just a momentary smile but a deep, new joy. It will be a bubbling experience of new hope that puts a brightness in your eyes and a song in your heart.

In the midst of the darkness you will learn lessons you might never have learned in the day. We all have seen dreams turn to ashes—ugly things, hopeless experiences—but beauty for ashes is God's exchange. Offer yourself to God and ask for a spirit of praise so your whole being will be restored.

Sorrows come, but each time God will be there to remind you that HE CARES. Romans 8:28 means God causes all things in our lives to work together for good. Remember:

Compost makes great gardens.

God is offering Himself to you daily, and the rate of exchange is fixed: your sins for His forgiveness, your hurt for His balm of healing, your sorrow for His joy. Give Him your pain. Give him the guilt you feel, the heartaches that come to us all. They are part of living, but if you focus on Jesus Christ, He alone can ease your heartache. Then He uses us to dry the tears of others.

Many of us are in God's waiting room—and it seems we've been here FOREVER. But you do meet such interesting people there—wonderful people who are also learning lessons as they suffer and grow. You are not alone; *thousands* like you are trying to find some relief from nights of loneliness.

It takes a long, long time for the deep hurts to be resolved—sometimes it feels like forever. Hang in there! As someone said, genuine healing is not a microwave process. It's more like a Crock-pot experience.

The best vitamin for making friends: B1.[13]

Talking is sharing,
But listening is caring.

When one door closes, another door always opens—but those long hallways are a real drag.[14]

Medical Definitions from the Home for the Bewildered:
Artery: The study of painting
Bacteria: Back door of a cafeteria
CAT scan: Search for kitty

Amazing! If you hang something in a closet for a while, it shrinks two sizes.[15]

Dear God, please give me longer arms or put my feet higher, perhaps at my knees, so I can take off my shoes without feeling as though I'm about to give birth.[16]

In our youth we want to change the world. In old age, we want to change the youth.

One who is filled with joy preaches without preaching.

There are three ways to get something done:
1. Do it yourself.
2. Hire someone to do it.
3. Forbid your kids to do it.

Things to do today:
1. Get up
2. Survive
3. Go to bed.[17]

Sometimes God calms the storm, and sometimes He lets the storm rage and calms His child.[18]

May the God of hope fill you with all joy and peace as you trust in Him, so that you may overflow with hope by the power of the Holy Spirit.[19]

3

Pack Your Bags—
We're Going on a Guilt Trip

What should I wear today—
guilt, grief, shame, or multi-misery?

*A*fter shock and isolation, GUILT is the most common feeling endured by hurting parents who land on the ceiling when bad news hits. We know that Erma Bombeck says guilt is "the gift that keeps on giving." It is also a bit like the yeast the pioneers used in the olden days.

Back then, yeast was a very important commodity, something you couldn't just run to the corner store and buy. But people didn't hoard their yeast; they shared it with others because they knew if they just kept a little bit it would continue to swell and GROW until they had replaced what they had given away.

Guilt is like yeast. You can give away up to 90 percent of your guilt, and the 10 percent that is left will just keep on growing and growing until you have another BIG batch.

Many hurting parents feel guilty about what's happened to their children, believing that somehow something they did caused the problem. I've had my own struggles with this "gift." When our son Steve was killed in Vietnam, all I could think of was that I had signed papers allowing him to enlist in the marine corps a couple of months early—before his eighteenth birthday. It didn't help at all to realize that he would have enlisted ANYWAY as soon as he was old enough.

And when our oldest son, Tim, was killed in a car crash on his way home from Alaska, I thought, *Why didn't I INSIST that he ship his car by boat and FLY home instead?* (As if he would have listened to me!)

And after our son Larry disappeared into the homosexual lifestyle, all I could do was relive all the angry things I had said to him when we first learned he was gay. I was convinced my words had driven him away.

My mail tells me I'm not alone in feeling guilty. It seems that parents everywhere stagger backward from catastrophic news, wondering, *How could this happen?* Sadly, the answer that immediately pops into our minds is, *I must have done something WRONG! Where did I fail?*

That's when the guilt sets in—and guilt tortures us with its own special kind of misery. As one mother wrote, "The questions we have asked ourselves and the guilt sticks we have beaten ourselves with have done nothing except knock our smug answers out of our heads." Wracked with "whys" and immersed in "if onlys," we feel like the man who said:

SOMETIMES MY MIND IS SO UNCOMFORTABLE,
I WISH I COULD GO SOMEWHERE AND TAKE IT OFF.
Ashleigh Brilliant
Pot-shot #2960 © 1983

Many of the letters I receive are steeped with guilt. But sometimes I think my mail is a lot like life—abundantly rich but somehow WRONG! After all, most of the people who write are Christians who are well aware of the basic teaching of our faith: No matter WHAT we have done—whether or not we somehow did something to cause the current catastrophe—Jesus died to erase it from our slates. It's GONE!

Spatula Ministries is a pretty "low-tech" organization. Our office equipment consists of an IBM Selectric typewriter, a photocopier, and, most importantly, a Sony tape eraser. We use a lot of audio tapes, and when we have a garbled tape or one that's full of something that's no longer timely, we put it in the tape eraser, and *ZAP!* No matter how messed up the old tape was, in just a few seconds, we have a clean, brand-new tape with nothing on it. That's what God does when we come to Him and ask for forgiveness. First John 1:9 promises, "If we confess our sins, he is faithful and just to forgive us our sins, and to cleanse us from all unrighteousness" (KJV).

God CLEANSES us and makes us new. I like to say the one thing God CANNOT see is our sin because it is covered by the blood of Jesus. We are FORGIVEN—and as Christians we KNOW it! Many of us have been taught this foundational principle since childhood. Since our days as toddlers at Vacation Bible School we've been singing the old chorus, "Gone, gone, gone, gone, yes my sins are gone!"[1]

But sadly, this wonderful message sometimes seems to be written on our hearts in magical ink that somehow disappears when the conditions are right. And when it does, God's eternal promise actually seems to cause hurting parents MORE pain—because they find themselves unable to accept it. As one mother wrote:

> It's been a struggle to forgive myself for my failures as a parent. I've lived with feelings of failure and guilt so long I forgot Jesus died for that, and because I did not accept His forgiveness and cleansing I've spent months beating up myself. I keep trying to carry the burden alone.

Another wrote:

> Your comments on guilt gave me insight on what to do with the guilt. It is wonderful to hear it is not my fault and that I shouldn't get caught up in the guilt, but no one ever told me what I could do with it! Yes, the answer is simplistic, but giving my guilt over to God just wasn't something I thought about

doing. I am grateful that I am now able to begin to comprehend God's unconditional love, His unfailing love for His children.

Consider Yourself Hugged!

"Suzy's Zoo" illustration © 1992 Suzy Spafford.
Used by permission.

And still another said:

> Barbara, we can't figure it out. Of course we say, "Where did we go wrong?" and all the other things parents always wonder. We have all been to a Christian counselor, but I don't know that it helped. I pray every day and am truly trying to turn the situation over to the Lord, but in my heart and mind I still worry. . . .

Guilt creates a vicious circle that's hard to escape. As one troubled Christian said:

> I FEEL SO GUILTY
> ABOUT FEELING GUILTY!

One woman asked:

> How do I learn to not be so concerned with what other people think? I'm ashamed and embarrassed to tell my friends, coworkers, and family about what's happened to us. It's probably a "guilt thing," worrying about what they think of ME, not my son. As if I didn't do something right when I was raising him or as if I'm partly to blame.

Another said she felt like her forehead had been TATTOOED with the word *FAILURE.* And still another wrote:

> We wonder where we went wrong with our daughter—what can we do, etc. I love the Lord, but sometimes I can hardly pray. I have been too ashamed to tell anyone, so there is really no one to talk to.

Learning to Accept God's Gift

The truth is, sometimes it's an effort to receive God's forgiveness. We have to make a conscious decision to ACCEPT

Christ's cleansing as a wonderful, expensive, sacrificial GIFT. I like the way one mother said she adapted something from one of my books to do this:

> Barbara, your picture of the mother climbing the steps and giving her present [the gift-wrapped box containing her child] to Jesus has been a very healing image for me. I've had to climb those stairs many times, but each time I feel a great sense of peace and relief.
>
> The picture prompted me to imagine another scene that's also helped:
>
> I imagine Jesus bringing a big, gift-wrapped box to ME. In my "scenario" He rings my doorbell, and I find Him standing on my porch (sort of like a heavenly UPS man, I guess). He smiles at me so kindly and hands me the box.
>
> I open it and find a bottle of special "perfume." (Barbara, it's that GUILT-AWAY spray of 1 John 1:9 you told about in your book.) As I squirt it all over myself, I feel a wonderful tingling. It makes me so happy I laugh and dance and shout for joy.
>
> Jesus stands there watching me enjoy His present, and the smile I see on His face is another part of the gift I receive: As I use what He has given me, I bring *Him* joy—and that, in turn, makes me happy too!
>
> When I feel myself sinking into the guilt pit, I find a quiet place and close my eyes. Then I imagine the doorbell ringing . . .

After you've sprayed yourself with "Guilt-away" perfume and wiped your past clean with the windshield wiper of God's love, you can take a sniff of God's "laughing gas" by breathing in the promise of Psalm 32:1:

> What HAPPINESS for those whose guilt has been forgiven!

What JOYS when sins are covered over!
What RELIEF for those who have confessed their
sins and God has cleared their record.[2]

Something that happened to me recently let me feel all
those emotions. We had a dear neighbor who had LOTS of
cats (at one time there were FORTY!). She was eighty-four
years old, and we sort of looked after her, and I did her shopping and bought tons of cat food.

We loved her and felt close to her, but after she died last
year I was shocked to learn she left me two gorgeous sparkling
diamond rings! What an unexpected sparkle in my life!

I had the rings sized and wore them proudly—until someone suggested that "anyone who has a tax-exempt, nonprofit
ministry shouldn't have expensive diamonds like that!" Talk
about guilt trips!

But after I thought about it awhile I decided it was okay to
wear the beautiful rings if I tell folks they were a GIFT, and
after all, their sparkles remind me of how God brings such
unexpected joys into my life. So if you see me on some TV
show or video or at a conference and I'm wearing those rings,
you'll know where they came from. How I thank the Lord for
the special ways He encourages us to "keep on keeping on"!

Bill, who has one of those melancholy personalities that
causes him to see the dark cloud inside every silver lining,
says that I EARNED every sparkle in the rings for all the cat
doo-doo I cleaned up and all those heavy (industrial size)
bags of cat food I hefted. But I think of them as special
sparkles for one who is undeserving of such a gift.

Dealing with Mistakes

When we're trying to get rid of our guilt feelings, and
while we struggle to remember that principle I stress so
strongly—"where there is no control there is no responsibility"—we must also be honest with God about what we
have done wrong. After all, we ALL make mistakes.

We must deal with past actions, accept any failures, and
acknowledge that we are (gasp!) NOT PERFECT! We must

relinquish our failures to God—reach out and hand them over. THEN WE STAND CLEAN BEFORE THE LORD!

Remember, God believes you are worth loving, even with your sins . . . even with your shameful past . . . even with your rebellion.

Even if you were the only sinner in the world, God loves you so much Jesus would have died for you alone! GOOD NEWS! He was nailed to a cross so YOU CAN STOP NAILING YOURSELF TO A CROSS! Work at it until you get it down pat: Accept His forgiveness and live a guilt-free life from here on out!

"THAT'S THE TV REMOTE CONTROL YOU'RE HOLDING, NOT THE GARAGE DOOR OPENER."

© 1990 John McPherson. Used by permission of John McPherson. Included in *McPherson's Marriage Album* (Grand Rapids: Zondervan, 1991).

A Drop of Water in a Pond of Blessings

Sometimes we feel guilty because of our attitudes and expectations. To be honest, I would have to admit that of our four sons, I really expected Barney, our youngest, to bring us the most grief. After all, he's the one who painted the floor of the neighbor's porch BLACK and accumulated TWENTY-

TWO PARKING TICKETS before he was eighteen! I couldn't imagine, back then, that I would ever come home from a trip, as we did last year, and find a note like this waiting for us:

> Mom & Dad,
>   I just wanted to tell you how much I love you! Thanks for all the things you do for me. . . . I am so proud to have Barbara Johnson as my mom and Gopher Bill for my dad. . . . I can't tell you how thankful I am for my mom and dad and everything we've been through, your trust in me, your belief in me. Your support and love have made and molded me to be the person I am today! I'm going to, with God's help, do the same for others.
>
> Love,
> Barney

I was really beaming about this "love letter" until I read the last line:

> P.S. I got another speeding ticket! Ain't it great!

We have to share some of the credit for Barney's "molding" (except his driving habits) with his wife, Shannon, our darling "daughter-in-love" for eighteen years. But since this book is about hearing bad news and learning to live with heartache, I must share what I once considered really BAD news about Barney. My reaction to this situation was something I felt guilty about for a long time.

If you've read my other books, you may remember that Barney was the darling baby I brought home on Christmas morning in a little red, fuzzy stocking, and he was so beautiful—the only pretty baby I ever had. But he had colic, and if he had been FIRST, he would have been my LAST baby!

Barney's real name is Dean, after my dad. He got his nickname because we used to have a player piano with a piano roll that played "Barney Google, with the goo-goo-googly eyes." Barney played that song until we all went a bit goofy, but it fits him to a T.

He went to Christian schools and had to learn Scripture verses each week that became the bane of MY existence because he balked so much at learning them. I would sit him down on the bed while I was getting myself ready for work, or I would make him sit at the kitchen table while I was cooking supper and make him recite the verse and the "address" of the verse . . . and just suffer along with him as he tried to learn his Scripture verses for school.

Barney accepted the Lord when he was just a little fellow and was baptized and went through all the motions, but when he was in high school, after Tim was killed, we saw him slipping away—discovering hints of marijuana and beer in his car.

He had no big problems with school or behavior, but out of our concern, we talked with his high school counselor. He told us Barney's goals were "to have a windmill and pump gas from his own gas pump." The counselor assured us that those were not bad goals for the way some kids were thinking at the time. So, since Barney was such a fun-loving and agreeable guy at home, we figured he was a typical teenager, and we knew that losing Tim was a big blow to him. Barney had been especially close to him and followed him around like a little brother does.

One day Barney came in and showed me a picture of a darling little brown-eyed gal named Shannon. Up to this time his interests had been in dirt-bike riding, cheeseburgers, and collecting trophies for championship motocross contests. So I was glad to see his choice of such a precious girl. I asked the usual questions about where she was from, how he met her, and, of course, I assumed she was a Christian.

BUT I WAS WRONG!

He told me right off that she didn't go to any church and was definitely NOT a Christian. It was as if he was, for the first time, asserting himself . . . and waiting for my response.

Now, you must realize that Barney held all our hope and prospects of having a Christian family—and GRANDKIDS! Steve was gone. Tim was gone. Larry was out doing his thing in the gay lifestyle. So Barney was *our only hope!* For him to tell me he was IN LOVE with this girl who was not a Christian—well, you can imagine how hard it was for me not to explode with dismay!

It simply was not possible for me to think of Barney marrying a girl who was unsaved and had no church background. Inside, I fussed and fumed, obsessed with the fact that my son was dating a HEATHEN and imagining that they would probably have children and raise them without letting us have any spiritual input. How unthinkable that our special Barney would get involved with a non-Christian! To me, this news was like number thirteen on a disaster scale of one to ten (ten being the worst)!

Barney knew from his training how we felt, and I knew HE was a Christian, although his teenage behavior was not what we wanted. We knew kids have to experiment and go through phases . . . but there was just no way we could see him marrying a girl who wasn't a Christian!

But what could we do? How could I, being just his mother, bring about a change? Could I just sit back and wait for a bolt from heaven to bring this miracle? Could I just watch and pray and be a witness for the Lord? I remembered the old song that said, "Sing and smile and pray . . . that's the only way. If you sing and smile and pray, you'll drive the clouds away."[3] Well, that sounded fine, but how was that going to get this darling Shannon to know the Lord?

Somehow I had to put some "feet" on my prayers, and the time was getting short. Shannon was coming over to our house frequently, and I could tell their relationship was getting serious. She had a little blue Volkswagen, and when I would come home and see it parked there, I would pray desperately for God to SHOW me some way to lead her to the Lord. Sure, I knew all the four spiritual laws and knew Scripture verses and the simple ways to share Christ, but somehow I also knew that Barney would resent my starting in with all THAT. So I prayed for another way . . .

At that time, wonderful Christian concerts were happening on Saturday nights at Calvary Chapel in Costa Mesa. All the young people I knew (except Barney) loved to go, and a couple thousand kids would sing and listen to the message, and it was a real lighthouse for young people. I thought, *This is it!* So I invited Shannon to go with me to the concert. In fact, I invited her several times, and each time she said she was too busy.

But finally, one night she reluctantly agreed to go with me. To make it more palatable, I promised her we would eat at a special place down near the chapel that I knew she would love.

At the concert the music was deafeningly loud for me, but she loved it, and I sensed a real hunger in her as she listened to Greg Laurie give the message. At the conclusion, she bounded down the aisle and knelt at the front of the auditorium with tears openly flowing down her cheeks! She accepted the Lord right there at the concert! Her immediate love for Jesus was genuine and total. Her heart was so open to the gospel message.

Like I said, I used to feel guilty about the way I felt about Shannon when we first met her—because it turned out that she has been one of the best things that ever happened to our family—and to a lot of other people. Her coming to the Lord was like throwing a little stone in a big pond. The next week she took her mother and sister to the concert, and they both accepted the Lord. And the following week she took her grandmother and great-grandmother, and both of them went forward and came to Christ. And since then Shannon has been the instrument God has used to bring MANY, MANY people to know the Lord.

Just this week as I was preparing this manuscript, she called to tell me about someone she had led to the Lord several years ago. She had just had a call telling her *that* person, in turn, had brought several others to the Lord.

Shannon is perfectly described by that verse in Daniel that says, "Those who turn many to righteousness will glitter like stars forever."[4] Shannon is truly a shining star in our lives; I like to say she has poked many holes in others' darkness.

Now that she and Barney have two precious teenage girls of their own, Kandee and Tiffany, I had to wonder how she would respond if she learned one of them was seriously involved with a non-Christian. When I posed the question to her, she replied, "Oh, Barb! We just could NOT have that! I would just die!"

Well, I certainly know how she felt and what she meant. But I also know Shannon would take the steps necessary to make that change possible, because I've seen her do it before. Her life has been a witness to Barney, so much so that now both of them are totally dedicated to the Lord, and they have raised their children to love God. They have taught them His Word and His promises, soundly grounding them in the Bible principles.

I know mothers-in-law can be a pain. They say that:

> Mixed emotions are having your mother-in-law
> drive over a cliff in your new Cadillac!

But my relationship with Shannon is truly one of love. Sometime when I think about it, I'm overwhelmed by how much joy Shannon—the subject of that blast of bad news so many years ago—has brought to our lives. Not a week goes by that she doesn't brighten my life with some little sparkle. Last week she gave me a beautiful Norman Rockwell plaque showing a darling little boy kneeling beside his bed, saying his prayers. The note she enclosed said,

> My dearest Mom-in-Love,
>   This little boy praying by his bedside just reached out and grabbed my heartstrings. I wanted this to be a small gift of thanks for something you've done that I don't think I could ever thank you enough for.

> Thank you, Barb, for teaching your little boy to pray
> and to hide God's Word in his heart, which became
> a blessing to me as his wife.

What a day-brightener that was! As I read her note and looked at that precious little boy saying his prayers, I couldn't help but think back to all those hours Barney and I spent struggling to memorize all those Scripture verses. And now, thirty years later, his wonderful WIFE is thanking me for it! If I'd known things would work out so well I would surely have been more patient!

And while I'm talking about how delightful Shannon is, I would be remiss if I didn't add that she and her parents had a few doubts of their own when they were getting to know Barney. For starters, there was the time she and her parents decided to drop by our house unannounced so her folks could meet Barney—and he answered the door in his boxer shorts!

And his method of proposing probably wasn't much more reassuring to them: He showed up at their house with the engagement ring he planned to give Shannon dangling from his ear on AN EARRING!

All these things just about sent all of us into orbit back then, but now they've become memories we can laugh about. One of my favorite memories is the way Shannon describes that moment at the concert when Greg Laurie said, "Any of you who want to ask Jesus into your life tonight, I want you to get up and come down here right now." Shannon says:

> Suddenly it was as if an invisible hand picked up
> the back of my blouse. I felt like I was floating down
> to the front of the church. I wanted Jesus more than
> anything I'd ever wanted before. I asked Him into
> my life. And I wanted MORE of what I had found
> there—that was such a Spirit-filled place.
>
> And as I stood there in the front of the church I
> turned to look back at Barb, and she had this huge,

joyous smile on her face like she was thinking, *MIS-SION ACCOMPLISHED!*

When I think of the joy Shannon has brought into our lives, I regret all that time I spent worrying about the way things would turn out. I should have remembered the plaque that hangs in my Joy Room.[5] It says:

BARBARA...

TRUST ME.

I HAVE
EVERYTHING
UNDER
CONTROL.

Jesus

Learning to Laugh at Crazy Calamities
When we're able to relinquish ALL our problems, ALL our worries, and ALL our sins to the Lord, we are free to live the

guilt-free lives He planned for us. God can help you find the SONshine inside yourself so you can laugh again. No matter where you are, He is with you, and as someone said:

I WOULD RATHER WALK WITH GOD IN THE DARK THAN GO ALONE IN THE LIGHT.

One mother wrote to say, "Each of us is in various stages of recovery from WHATEVER, and it's important that we are able to laugh along the way. It's kept me from insanity numerous times. . . . Out of your heartache comes something beautiful that God has/is/will use . . ."

Of course, even though God forgives us all our sins, we still have to do some earthly explaining from time to time. I remember when that happened to me many years ago during one of my pregnancies. It was back in the Dark Ages when doctors wanted pregnant women to limit their weight gain to only fifteen pounds or so, and they were SO STRICT about everything.

It was a real problem for me because I can gain fifteen pounds by just WALKING past a bakery. (My fat cells apparently absorb the fumes right through my skin—I don't even have to swallow!)

Luckily, on my first visit to this obstetrician, I noticed that the scale was next to a windowsill. So when I would go in to be weighed I would secretly put my finger down on this sill next to the scale and PUSH . . . and it would make me seem to weigh four or five pounds less.

Then one day I went in, and to my SHOCK they had painted the room and moved the scale out in the middle of the floor, away from the windowsill! I had no place to push so I would weigh less. When the nurse weighed me it looked like I had gained about ten pounds in only a couple of weeks!

The doctor threw a FIT and immediately demanded to know what I had been doing, what I had been eating, what had happened that had caused such a big gain. He was incredulous!

So I finally had to tell him that my weight gain was HIS fault because he had had the room painted and the scale had been moved away from the windowsill out into the middle of the floor.

I guess the moral of the story is that my sins will always find me out. But even when they do . . .

> GOD LOVES ME SO MUCH
>   THAT HE WILL ACCEPT ME
>   JUST AS I AM . . .
>   BUT HE LOVES ME TOO MUCH
>   TO LEAVE ME THAT WAY!

In other words, God loves us too much to leave us stuck to the ceiling! Of course, sometimes it hurts to be peeled off the ceiling, and sometimes it's not immediately apparent that we've "landed" in a better situation. As one woman wrote, "We've fallen off the ceiling, flat on the floor."

Another woman who experienced a similar plunge said, "Right now I don't need a Spatula. I need a backhoe!" Still another said, "I didn't have to be scraped off the ceiling, but my heart had to be taken up off the floor since it was pulled out when our son told us he was gay."

I guess it's times like these when we start thinking

> MOST OF MY PROBLEMS EITHER HAVE NO
> ANSWER OR ELSE THE ANSWER IS WORSE
> THAN THE PROBLEM!
>   Ashleigh Brilliant
>   Pot-shot #2101 © 1981

We need to put things into eternal perspective and remember the promise of Romans 8:28 that God makes *everything*— even calamities—work for our good. Sometimes it's awfully hard to wait for the "good" to "work." And every now and then, as we feel like we're plunging to ever-greater depths, we can't help but wonder if anything good will really come out of our misery. As one woman said,

I know these trials are supposed to make
me strong—but I'm not sure I WANT to be a
SAMSON!

Just remember, no matter how far you plummet:

The Lord lifts the fallen
and those bent beneath their loads.[6]

So, as the writer of Hebrews advises, "take a new grip
with your tired hands, stand firm on your shaky legs, and
mark out a straight, smooth path for your feet so that those
who follow you, though weak and lame, will not fall and
hurt themselves but become strong."[7] And if all else fails to
boost your spirits and strengthen your "shaky legs," you
may have to resort to "random acts of silliness" such as deco-
rating your bumper with a big, bold bumper sticker like the
one I saw recently:

WARNING: I KNOW KARATE!
(and three other Chinese words)

Lay your guilt aside, fill your heart with the comfort of
God's love and mercy—and find something to laugh about!

I always get a laugh out of the way people get
confused about the silly titles of my books. For
example, one woman recently referred to *Stick a
Geranium in Your Hat and Be Happy* as *Stick a
Geranium in Your Cranium.*

But my all-time favorite came from a reader who was referring to *Mama, Get the Hammer, There's a Fly on Papa's Head.* He wrote, "I just last night was reading your book, *Hit Grandpa on the Head, He's Still Breathing!*

Bumper Sticker: BLESSINGS HAPPEN!

It is bad to suppress laughter. It goes back down and spreads to your hips.[8]

I'm pleased to share one of my favorite recipes, sent by a letter-writer who knows my fondness for goofy gumbo and flake cake:

Easy Recipe for Elephant-Broccoli Stew

1 medium-sized elephant
1 ton coarsely chopped broccoli
(salt and pepper to taste)
2 rabbits (optional)

Cut elephant into bite-size pieces (takes about two months). Add coarsely chopped broccoli and seasonings. Cover with water. Cook in large kettle over open fire for about four weeks. If unexpected guests show up, two rabbits may be added (but only do this if necessary since nobody likes to find a HARE in their stew). Serves approximately thirty-five hundred people.

George Burns's "grooming tip for the over-ninety set": Take care not to wear stripes that are out of sync with your wrinkles.[9]

God gave us memories
so that we might have roses in December.

Families with babies
and families without babies
are sorry for each other.[1]

If you treat every situation
as a life-and-death matter . . .
You will die a lot.

Oh Lord,
    Bless the person who is too busy to worry in the daytime and too sleepy to worry at night.[11]

One of Satan's proudest accomplishments:
the "hold" button on modern telephones.

We probably wouldn't worry about what people
think of us if we could know how seldom they do.[12]

But as for me,
I will always have hope.[13]

I Thought I Had a Handle on Life,
But Then It Fell Off

Something to hang on to when your world falls apart.

Did you ever see that episode of *I Love Lucy* where Lucy gets stuck in the freezer and can't get the door open? When she finally emerges, she has icicles dangling off her nose, her head, and her elbows, and her clothes are frozen solid. I thought of that silly image when a friend of mine, the PTA president at her daughter's school, told me about a nightmare experience she had recently when she was helping serve soft drinks during the school's annual field day.

All day long the dedicated PTA mothers worked outside in the blistering heat of a June day in Florida, hurriedly pouring drinks for the sweltering students, who flocked to the booth for refreshments after competing in the various events.

At one point my friend, Sue, was dispatched to the school's kitchen to get another bag of ice. No one was in the kitchen, but she found the massive, six-inch-thick door of the huge, walk-in freezer, stepped inside, and flipped on the light.

It felt so good in the freezer after spending several hours in the ninety-degree heat that, even though she was in a hurry, Sue stopped a moment to close her eyes and soak in the sweet coolness of the frosty air. Then she found the ice and turned toward the door.

"My heart stopped," she said. "There was no handle on the door! It was just a big, smooth, metal slab set into the wall. I couldn't imagine how I could get out. I tried to get my fingers in the crack between the door and the wall so I could pull on the door, but it fit too tightly. Then I saw a little lever on the wall next to the door. I shoved the lever up and down, thinking it might somehow open the door, but nothing happened—absolutely nothing.

"I exploded into full-bore panic. I thought how ironic it was going to be to freeze to death on such a hot day. I wondered how long it would be before any of the other mothers missed me—and how long it took to die in a freezer.

"Even though I knew no one was in the kitchen, I started shouting for help and rapping on the door with my knuckles, screaming to make myself heard. I figured at least the exertion might keep me warm for a little while.

"Suddenly the door swung inward and nearly knocked me down. The custodian stood there with this strange look on his face. I was so relieved I burst into tears and said, 'Oh, thank you, thank you, thank you! I was so scared!'

"He looked at me with that same strange look and said, 'Why? What happened?'

"I said excitedly, 'I couldn't get out! I couldn't get the door open. There's no handle!'

"The custodian smiled a gentle little smile and motioned for me to step back into the freezer. He came in with me, and then he gave the door the smallest little *push*, and it easily swung outward. 'Look,' he said, 'it's a *swinging* door. You don't need a handle—you just *push*.'"

A lot of hurting parents know exactly how it feels to find themselves frozen in "full-bore panic" with no means of escape. What a blessing it is, then, to have someone come alongside us and show us a simple way out of our misery.

That's what I want to do in this chapter—share some of the ideas that other parents have used to find their way off the ceiling, up from the pit, through the fire—or out of the freezer. Sometimes the ideas seem simple—like a gentle push

on a swinging door—but even the simplest acts can make a
world of difference to a parent in pain.

**Life is an adventure. Hang on to your hat
and scream for all you're worth!**

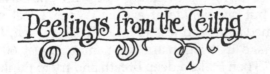

Peelings from the Ceiling

When one door of happiness closes, another
opens. But often we look so long at the closed
door that we do not see the one that has been
opened for us.[1]

Surviving One Minute at a Time

As you might expect, one of my favorite "lifesavers" is using humor to hammer out the hurts. I'm always thankful—and a little amazed—when parents can latch on to this "handle" early in their grief, as did this mother, who wrote me two letters in less than two weeks:

December 2
Dear Barbara,

I feel like I have just been hit by a Mack truck. My son has been living the gay lifestyle for several years. . . . We have always been very close, but this last year he hasn't been home twice. He came to see me two days ago. He skirted the issue at first, saying he felt fine, but eventually he cried out that he had just found out he was HIV positive. I'm so worried. . . . It would be very much in character for him to let me down easy and not tell me the whole story. I'm afraid he already has AIDS.

December 12
Dear Barbara,

Thank you for your phone call after you received my letter.

My son has since been diagnosed as already having AIDS.

These days I am dealing not with one day at a time, but *one minute* at a time. When I feel overwhelmed with sadness or grief, I tell myself, "You can make it through the next minute, just 60 seconds." Then I take a deep breath and try to think that *today* I should really be rejoicing because right now, today, *this minute*, our son is still alive for us to love and enjoy. Why destroy the rest of the time we have left by being miserable through to the end? It's hard, in fact it *feels* impossible, to have to let go. But just for this one minute I'm not going to deal with that.

P.S. I went to the grocery store today and noticed a poster showing a picture of a hot-fudge sundae. Just above the sinfully delicious-looking sundae, it said, "CHEAPER THAN THERAPY." I had to smile at that—went home and made myself a bowl of therapy!

This darling mom WILL make it through because she has found HUMOR to flatten out her pain. Can you see the change between her two letters? She also realizes the value of ACCEPTANCE, and she's dealing with her situation ONE MINUTE AT A TIME. If only others could learn this valuable lesson so early in the game!

There is a thin line that separates laughter and pain, comedy and tragedy, humor and hurt. And how do you know laughter if there is no pain to compare it with?²

Sometimes it seems we're unable to cross that line from pain to joy because we can't see the line! Our lives are too cluttered with painful experiences to even know it's there. If that's your situation . . . let go! Turn loose!

Bruce Larson tells a story about a man who was taking a cruise on an ocean liner. Somehow one of his socks got away from him and blew over the railing, forever lost. Without a thought, the man flipped the other sock over the railing too, then stretched out on the chaise lounge and took a nap. He knew when he was looking at a hopeless situation, and he wasn't about to let it ruin his opportunity for pleasure.

In contrast, many of us would take the remaining sock home and KEEP it, hoping a mate might miraculously turn up sometime. But all we would be doing is cluttering up our sock drawer. Instead, like the man on the ship, we need to let go of the painful situations that are out of our control and step out, unencumbered, knowing God holds our future in His hands.

Our lives can become so cluttered with all the stuff we insist on hanging on to—both physical (like single socks and broken gadgets) and emotional (like guilt and pain and misery). I saw a little essay by an unknown writer that described all the stuff that clutters our lives: closet stuff, drawer stuff, attic stuff, basement stuff, good stuff, bad stuff, food stuff, cleaning stuff, medicine stuff, clothes stuff, outside stuff, stuff to make us smell better and look younger, stuff to make us look healthier, stuff to hold us in or fill us out, stuff to read, stuff to play with, stuff to entertain us, little stuff, big stuff, useful stuff, and junky stuff.

The essay ends with this happy reminder: "Now when we leave all our stuff and go to heaven, whatever happens to our stuff won't matter. We will still have the good stuff God has prepared for us in heaven."

Light for the Next Step

When we can get rid of some of the senseless clutter that burdens our lives, we can start moving again, even if all we can take is baby steps toward recovery. Verdell Davis, in her book *Riches Stored in Secret Places,* talks about moving through grief one slow step at a time. She describes the monasteries of ancient Europe where "the monks walked the dark hallways with candles secured to the toes of their shoes, giving light only for the next step."

As she grieved for her husband, Creath, who had died in a plane crash, she eventually came "to grasp the meaning of light for the next step—as [the monks] walked, the light always went just before them."

Even while she wondered why God "could not light the way a little more brightly when we are so consumed with pain and fear," she learned that in her journey through grief, "the candle on the toe of each shoe is really enough. Because God Himself is the candle."[3]

In God's economy, nothing is wasted—not one flicker of hope, not a single act of kindness, not one imponderable "Why?" And in the darkest pit of despair, when God gives us the light to take only one step at a time, His message to us is still simply:

Trust Me.

God knows what He is doing. I believe what He said to the Jews when they were in captivity also applies to believers today when we face hopeless situations. Through Jeremiah, God told the miserable people:

> FOR I KNOW THE PLANS THAT I HAVE FOR YOU, . . . PLANS FOR WELFARE AND NOT FOR CALAMITY TO GIVE YOU A FUTURE AND A HOPE.[4]

Of course, sometimes the "plans" God has for us here on earth are not always the same ones we would have chosen for ourselves. In other words:

> This may be the answer to my prayers,
> but it's not the answer I was hoping for.
> > Adapted from
> > Ashleigh Brilliant
> > Pot-shot #3130 © 1983

If we can keep our minds open to the blessings, humor, and EDUCATION in whatever happens to us—if we can set that little invisible radar dish on top of our heads to constantly search for BLESSINGS instead of DISASTERS—our lives will be enriched by the experiences we endure and we can GROW from the calamities that fertilize our lives! I saw a little piece by an unknown writer that said, "We must try to take life moment by moment. The present moment is usually pretty tolerable if only we refrain from adding to its burden that of the past and the future."

Keep your
chin up...

"Suzy's Zoo" illustration © 1985 Suzy Spafford.
Used by permission.

Of course, when we've learned this important lesson—of
living one moment at a time—we then face ANOTHER problem. It's explained perfectly in the title of William Ferris's
book:

YOU LIVE AND LEARN,
THEN YOU DIE AND FORGET IT ALL![5]

Someday, everything will make sense. For now, we just have to concentrate on surviving each day, no matter *what* surprises it holds for us. As one friend wrote,

THIS MORNING I CRACKED OPEN AN EGG . . .
AND PANTYHOSE FELL OUT!

Helpful Hints from Hurting Parents
A friend told me about meeting a professional psychologist recently whose son had been killed only a few weeks before in a tragic sports accident. As the two women got acquainted, they shared the stories of their loved ones' deaths. My friend admitted to the psychologist that she felt a little awkward, not knowing what to say to her to offer comfort—after all, SHE was the COUNSELOR!

My friend said that in a strange way, she even felt a little envious of the other woman's education because she thought the psychologist probably knew exactly the RIGHT things—the BEST things—to say to help someone through the grieving process. She finally mumbled a few words and added, "I don't know what it's like for a counselor—I just know what it's like for a MOM to have to go through this."

© Shannon Johnson

The psychologist smiled a sad little smile and said, "I've probably read twenty-five books since my son died—professional books, Christian books, self-help books—and the only thing that has helped me is to read or hear from other mothers. They're the only ones who can really understand."

I felt the same way this counselor did when I first learned that our son, Larry, was a homosexual. In a hurry to pick up my sister and her husband at the airport, I was almost out the door when the phone rang. It was a friend, wanting to borrow Larry's *Basic Youth* notebook.

I hurried back to his bedroom, and as I lifted the notebook out of his dresser drawer, I saw beneath it a pile of homosexual magazines, pictures, and letters from other young men. At first glance, I thought it must be material for some sort of college research project (Larry had just graduated the night before from a local junior college). Then, in an instant, I knew that wasn't it at all. That's when my teeth started to itch, the shag rug somehow became jammed in my throat, and the elephant settled onto my chest.[6]

I desperately wanted to find another MOTHER of a homosexual—someone who had already been through the ordeal I was facing. But I couldn't find one. I called the crisis hot line and said, "My son is a h-h-h-h-h-homosexual" (I could hardly bring myself to say it, and the word "gay" was not used back then in that context), "and I want to talk to another mother of a h-h-h-h-h-homosexual!" I cried.

But the hot-line staff didn't have any mothers of homosexuals—all they could offer was to let me talk to another homosexual. But I already had one of those! I needed to hear from a MOTHER!

That was several years ago, and the world was a lot different then. For a long time I felt like ours was the only family on the face of the earth that had a homosexual child. Now it seems I don't know *any* families that don't have a homosexual somewhere in their midst! I've heard from THOUSANDS of mothers, and many of them write to share what has helped them work through their grief. Usually it's nothing profound—just a gentle *push* toward the road leading to wholeness. These are the moms who know:

> If you have your feet firmly on the ground
> and your head in the clouds,
> you're walking in a fog.[7]

In the next pages, I want to share some of these mothers' ideas for surviving devastating news. Some of these letters are full of anguish as well as help; to soften the blow I've sprinkled in some "peelings from the ceiling" to diffuse the pain and help you smile as you read. I hope in these parents' words you'll find a lifeline to pull yourself up from the depths of the cesspool.

From North Carolina:

I began my grief as you did, Barbara, by counting the roses on the bedroom wallpaper. Then one day, I took one second out of my counting and smiled at myself in the mirror. I added one second of smiling into the mirror every day until I was really smiling again, outside and inside.

Here are some other steps I took from your books:

1. Cried.

2. Moved toward happiness.

3. Started a Joy Box with small stuff.

4. Started a Joy ROOM with big stuff.

5. Gave myself a party with lots of games and prizes and showed a cartoon video before refreshments. (It made me happy to see others happy.)

6. Helped a friend and let her lean on me.

7. Sought help. It's crucial to find an ear that will listen, even if it is a paid ear.

8. Typed out what I underlined in your books.

9. Prayed/Bible study.

10. Thanked God even for sand-grain-size blessings.

The best thing about the future is that it comes one day at a time.

From Florida:

After reading all of your books I know that I must hand my daughter over completely to the Lord. Within forty-eight hours of reading your *Gloomees* book, my faith began returning. Since then I have said, "WHATEVER, LORD!" and have given her to God. For the first time in two and a half years, I feel stronger. My hopelessness has turned into HOPE![8]

From Michigan:

Five years have passed since our daughter and granddaughter died. Each year it gets a little better, but it will never be the same again. . . . My husband, son, and I have helped serve dinner to the needy on Thanksgiving and Christmas these last two years, and that has enabled us to survive. We are making new memories and establishing new traditions.

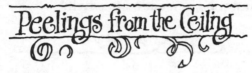

Remember, every cloud has a silver lining . . . And sometimes a bolt of lightning.

From Missouri:
My husband's confession that he had become involved with another woman threw me for a loop. He had ended the affair, and I forgave him immediately. But still, I was totally devastated. I even attempted suicide.

One evening my husband insisted that I go to our women's meeting at church to try to get back into life, and it was there that I heard the review of your book, *Stick a Geranium in Your Hat and Be Happy*. I thought it sounded great, but my husband certainly wasn't gay, and my children were great, so I didn't think it would apply to me. Three days later, I fell into my pit again and knew I had to do something. In the midst of a snowstorm, my husband drove me to our Christian bookstore to buy your book, and I hurried home to begin reading.

What a breath of fresh air! For the first time in three months, someone really could understand the heart-wrenching pain I was feeling. I'm still working on keeping the sock in my mouth when I want to say, "How could you!" again.

Peelings from the Ceiling

Blessed are they who have nothing to say and who cannot be persuaded to say it.[9]

From California:

My story is typical of a wayward son for fifteen years. Believing God for such a long time is hard but possible. For three years, our son hasn't contacted us, and we only hear little tidbits of heartache about him, but we choose to believe God's words of great promise to us.

I used your suggestions and three years ago when he left home, I turned his room into my Joy Room. I made a large, beautiful cross with lots of color and flowers and "nailed him there" (his picture) to see every time I enter. All around are fun things everywhere and "NO WHINING ALLOWED" signs. It's a joyful place, and I spend a lot of time there. It keeps hope alive and me well.

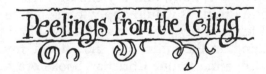

Peelings from the Ceiling

Hope is the feeling you have that the feeling you have isn't permanent.

From Alabama:

Barbara, until I read your books . . . I thought I was the only mother who had a gay child. I so need to hear from someone who has felt all the things only the mother of a gay child feels. Today was the first time since learning my son was gay that I have gone to church. I had withdrawn from the world, but after reading your books I realize I can't live this way.

I have done as you suggested. I have quit saying, "Why my son? Why me?" I start my day by saying, "WHATEVER, LORD!" And I have taken out my imaginary hammer and put my son on the cross with Jesus.

Be open-minded, but not so open-minded that your brains fall out.[10]

From West Virginia:

Barbara, you told me ten years ago that things would get better. I could hardly believe it then, but it's true!

From Texas:

I'm in my fourth year of therapy—four years of hell and pain and healing. That has been the hardest work I've ever done in my life. I had become completely isolated. I wouldn't see people. I wouldn't have anything to do with my husband. I hated myself and everything around me. As I dug myself out of the black pit I was in, I started to understand that God has been with me all along. I was never completely alone. . . . God was there preserving my life and my sanity. My healing continues. I still have not seen my son for twelve years. I still hurt so much I can hardly stand the pain, but I have God, and I have hope.

No matter how old she is, a mother watches her middle-aged kids for signs of improvement.[11]

From North Carolina:

We're still in life's parade, but limping. So much has happened—and HASN'T happened: The reunion long hoped for. The peace that passes all understanding. But I still keep hanging on to God's unconquerable promises that He can do the undoable.

So much "falling down" in life, isn't there? But thanks to a forgiving, enduring Lord who picks us back up with scraped elbows and a red sucker still stuck between our teeth! When it all looks impossible, we find somehow that we're eyeball to eyeball with yet another sunrise, refreshing our memories that it also rises to renew our hope.

Barbara, your humor, cheerful spirit, contented heart, and radiant hope form a rope I can swing on. Thanks for spreading joy to us parents of prodigals.

This last letter-writer's description of "limping" along in "life's parade" reminds me of a corollary joke someone sent me after I shared this old Irish proverb:

May those who love us, love us,
And those who don't love us,
May God turn their hearts.
And if He doesn't turn their hearts
May He turn their ankles,
So we can tell them by their limping.

My friend said those of us who have been "done wrong" by these "limping" jerks hold on to one hope:

TIME WOUNDS ALL HEELS.

Now let's look at some more letters offering *real* hope. Remember these are letter from *healing* parents sent with love to *freshly hurt* parents:

From Florida:
After a five-year homosexual relationship my daughter has moved back home! I see this as a second chance. I don't know what the outcome will be, but I am *hopeful*. Would you believe that the night before she called, after a long estrangement, I said to God, "God, I know You *can* change her, but *will* You?" I slept like a baby for the first time since all this began. Her phone call came the next morning.

I'm scared and hopeful at the same time—not pushing but praying harder than ever, trying to take each hour at a time.

From Georgia:
It's been four years of heartbreaking pain, loneliness, and emotional devastation, but God has turned my troubles into triumphs! I still shed my tears. I still miss my daughter and the others. But I now thank God every day for His blessings and His grace. Without God there is no life, no hope. With God there is everything!

From Indiana:

God used your books and you to lift me to a greater faith in Him and more self-esteem and joy than I've had in my entire life—I'm 56!

I've started a "mini-Spatula" ministry by myself. Just one-on-one with those who are hurting. I can't believe how many hurting people there are out there who, before my own pain (and your books), I just didn't see!

Now I make 45 copies of the *Loveline* newsletter and write notes on the top and mail them out to people I know who need a "splash of joy."

The great beautifier is a contented heart and a happy outlook.

From Michigan:

I have put my son in God's hands, as you suggested.

I have to love him from within only—it's all he will allow. But I will never NOT love him because, first, who am I to judge one of God's children, lest I be judged the same? Judgment is not my job (thank goodness!). And second, if I cannot love all here on earth as Jesus teaches, how can I expect a place with Him in heaven?

From Tennessee:

The one thing that has helped me is my faith in God—my Creator, Father, Savior, and Friend. I'm so glad He gives me a happy heart and laughing eyes to feel and see this mixed-up world I live in.

As I was getting prepped for surgery, they had given me medicine to relax me. When they came with the stretcher to take me to surgery, I decided I'd better use the bathroom. Because I was in La-La Land from the medicine, my husband helped me into the bathroom while the attendants and our pastor waited in the room. As I lifted my gown, I realized I had on my oldest underwear. I looked up at my husband and said, "Oh no! Mother told me to always wear my best underwear in case I was in an accident and had to go to the hospital!"

We just had a happy fit right there in the bathroom. I do not know to this day what our pastor and the attendants thought was going on in there, but laughter sure made my fears run away.

I am able to face the tornadoes in my life, not because I want to, because I would not choose this, but because God wants me to. So I know we are going to be fine.

This gal's letter just shows you can find humor anywhere—even a HOSPITAL BATHROOM! We all need to remember to look for the joy, no matter where we are when we find ourselves neck-deep in life's sludge because:

BEAUTIFUL FLOWERS CAN GROW ON DUNG HILLS.

MY MIND CONTAINS MANY GOOD IDEAS,
but it's not always easy to squeeze one out.
Ashleigh Brilliant
Pot-shot #3347 © 1985

Healing comes when you realize the light at the
end of the tunnel is NOT a train.[12]

A well-informed person . . .
Is somebody who has the same views and
opinions as yours.

Happy moments—those moments when you feel
fully alive—certainly exist. They swim by us
every day like shining, silver fish waiting to be
caught.[13]

As I love and encourage others . . .
I lift up Jesus,
I serve Jesus,
I imitate Jesus,
I, too, am blessed.[14]

Life is an endless struggle, full of frustrations
and challenges.
But eventually you find a hairstylist you like![15]

Thinking will get us to the foot of the mountain. Faith will get us to the top.

Human beings can live without air for a few minutes, without water for a week, without food for six weeks . . . and without a new thought for a lifetime!

The more you complain, the longer God lets you live.

Blessed are those . . . who walk in the light of your presence, O LORD.[16]

Answers We Didn't Wanna Hear to Questions We Didn't Wanna Ask

God only knows!

When I shared my home with five males—my husband Bill and our four young sons—I used to wonder what was so funny about the joke that asked:

Q: How many men does it take to change a
   bathroom-tissue roll?
A: Nobody knows. It's never been done!

Back then that riddle was just one of those little imponderable "whys" that kept life interesting. WHY couldn't anyone but Mom change the bathroom-tissue roll? There didn't seem to be an answer.

Of course, that was long before a lot more serious "whys" began wreaking havoc in our lives.

After Bill was so severely injured in an accident that his doctors declared him "unrehabilitatable" and told me he would be a vegetable the rest of his life, I asked a lot of whys. Why Bill? Why MY husband? After all, he was a good man, a patient father, a devoted Christian. I wondered why this had to happen to us, but I was so busy I didn't have time to dwell on the unanswerable questions.

I spent the next year caring for him (as well as our four boys) as we waited for a vacancy to open in the nearest veterans hospital, where he was to be admitted for a lifetime commitment. (The doctors didn't expect him to live longer than five years because of the blood clots in his brain.) During those months there seemed to be an endless variety of forms that had to be filled out and benefits such as Aid to the Blind, social security, veterans pension, etc., that had to be applied for.

And then, just as I got all the programs arranged and after we'd received twenty thousand dollars from the insurance company as compensation for his blindness, God healed Bill!

Of course we were all overjoyed that Bill was once again an active, loving member of the family. But that little "why?" kept creeping in as I thought of all those forms I'd filled out and the long lines I'd waited in. I was joyously thankful for God's healing touch, but I wondered WHY He couldn't have healed Bill BEFORE I got on all those programs![1]

**You are tuned to radio station W-H-Y,
broadcasting continuously, twenty-four hours a day,
from somewhere within your head.**

When Steven left for Vietnam, a new category of unanswerable questions opened up for us. The worst one began the day a U.S. Marines car stopped in front of our house and two officers in full-dress uniforms knocked at the door.

Steven's death was very difficult for us, and although we kept asking God, "Why? Why? Why?" we only heard silence— not the answer we, as devoted Christians, wanted to hear.

Eventually, though, we drew comfort from knowing Steven was our deposit in heaven. And our lives almost returned to normal . . . until the afternoon five years later when a phone call from the Royal Canadian Mounted Police informed us of Tim's death due to a drunk driver in the Yukon Territory.

While Steven's death had not been easy to accept, it had not been impossible. After all, he'd been in a war zone, and I had spent each anxious day since he'd left knowing that he *could* be killed. Tim's death, on the other hand, was a devastating shock. The call telling us he'd been killed came only a few hours after he'd called us himself from the Yukon, letting us know he was on his way home from Alaska.

With two sons dead, I wasn't just despondent, I was ANGRY. And a lot of my anger was directed straight toward God. For weeks after Tim's memorial service I drove to a nearby dump late every night so I could scream out my rage without Bill or our other two sons knowing about it. Sitting there overlooking the trash heap, I'd clinch my fists, pound on the steering wheel, and cry "WHY? WHY? WHY?" Hadn't we had enough pain with Bill's accident and Steve's death in Vietnam? How could God do this to us AGAIN? I already had one deposit in heaven; I didn't NEED another one. Why was God making us bear another loss like this? WHY?

Answers Don't Come, But Healing Does

The mail I get reassures me that I'm not the only hurting parent who ever raged at God, demanding to know WHY such pain had blown our lives off course. Here are just a couple of letters from anguished parents who found themselves dangling from unanswered questions:

> We have just learned that our daughter is involved in a lesbian lifestyle, and I have been experiencing everything you describe in *Geranium*. . . . For the first time I find my faith in God faltering.
>
> I lost another child many years ago to cancer and did not blame God; I found comfort in Him. But

this lesbian "thing" seems so perverse and unbelievable. I prayed for this child every day of her life and raised her in a Christian home. WHY WOULD GOD ALLOW HER TO GET INTO THIS MESS?!

I know there's no answer, but it has made it difficult to carry on with my Bible study, choir, etc.

ⓖ ⓖ ⓖ

Through reading the Bible and your books and doing some counseling we realized that our otherwise wonderful, sweet, caring child does not need our condemnation but rather our nonjudgmental love. But still we wonder, IS THIS REALLY GOD'S PLAN? We want so much to feel at peace about this—I guess it's a "give-it-to-God" problem once again.

ⓖ ⓖ ⓖ

Who knows what really goes on in our children's lives? ONLY GOD! . . . I can't believe what has happened—but for this we have JESUS.

Even when the answers don't come, if we can vent our grief, healing oozes almost unnoticed into our lives. It took a long time for it to come to us after Tim's death, but gradually our lives took on meaning again.

PEANUTS By Charles M. Schulz

PEANUTS reprinted by permission of
United Feature Syndicate, Inc. © 1995

Then, a year later, we were struck by Larry's announcement that he was a homosexual. This time I didn't wait until late at night; I did my screaming right away—at Larry. I quoted Scripture and cited God's laws and, worst of all, I told him, "I would rather have a son be DEAD than be a homosexual!"

My angry words drove him away from us, and shortly after that confrontation, Larry disappeared into the gay lifestyle for eleven years while I disappeared into our bedroom to count the roses on the wallpaper. Things got so bad that Bill was ready to commit me to the Home for the Bewildered, but our insurance wouldn't pay for it, so he decided to keep me at home since, as he told the doctor, I "wasn't vicious or anything."

More Medical Definitions from the Home for the Bewildered:

Clinical depression: The print your behind makes on the doctor's examination table.

Derange: Kitchen appliance. Usually sits right next to de fridge.

Bonding: What chewing gum does between your shoe and the pavement.

Repressing: What you'll be doing to your pants after a thirteen-hour car trip.

Healing process: Teaching your dog to walk beside you.[2]

Having cried my heart out, I resorted to a state of numbness. Occasionally I prayed, but all I seemed able to ask was the same old questions, "Why, God? Why MY son? Why ME?"

Finally I gave up, worn out from endlessly asking "Why?" and finally realizing I couldn't solve this problem or "fix Larry" by myself. Instead I imagined nailing Larry to the cross with Jesus. I gave the Lord my son and said, "WHATEVER, LORD! Whatever happens, he's YOUR child and You love him even more than I do, so I'm giving him to You, and WHATEVER happens he is Your child. Now I'm going to get on with my life.

A N S W E R S

PRICE LIST

Yes/No	**$ 1.00**
Where	**$ 1.25**
How	**$ 1.50**
Who	**$ 1.75**
Why (someone else's fault)	**$ 2.00**
Why (my fault)	**$20.00**

Dumb looks are still free.

Suddenly, I felt a tremendous release as if a million splashes of joy had somehow filled my heart. Since then I've tried to share with others the joy the Lord gave me in exchange for the burdens I had relinquished to Him.

Lessons from the Pit

In the years since I began saying "Whatever, Lord!" I've heard from other parents who have found the same relief by no longer asking God "Why?" and instead saying to Him, "Here! Take my child, Lord. I want what's best for this person I love so much, and that means giving him or her—and all the related problems—to YOU!"

These letters show how other "parents in the pit" have learned—and keep relearning—to do this:

> During the blackest period of my life I walked zombie-like into the market to buy food. I knew I had to go because there was no food left to eat in the house and although all I could do was lie in bed and cry, my husband wanted to eat and so did my dogs. Well, while standing at the checkout counter, I happened to look down near the *National Enquirer*, and there was your *Geranium* book. . . .
>
> Curiously, the night before I had prayed to God to help me, to give me strength, to give me SOMETHING. I had no more fight, no more will to live. I asked God to take my burdens in His hands because I could no longer handle them. Consequently, your book was sent to me by God. Nothing can convince me otherwise.
>
> Your book has helped me through my trial of a daughter who has literally broken my heart. You are right. There are yo-yo times. And the sun just keeps coming up every morning no matter what.
>
> P.S. If I didn't get so lost, I probably would have gone to the dump too.

ⓖ ⓖ ⓖ

It has been a long, painful process—letting go and letting God—but Barb, I am there at last. I do truly believe this is between my daughter and God. He will judge, and only He knows her pain and her struggles.

ⓖ ⓖ ⓖ

I owe you an apology! My young adult son tore my heart apart one vessel at a time, and I developed a hopelessness totally unfamiliar to me. As I was certainly "going down for the last time," my friend gave me *Stick a Geranium in Your Hat.*

I read your book with despair in my heart, . . . sure that you were most likely suffering in a huge box of denial. I even called you the "leader of La-La Land."

But I tasted your joy, and I am finally able to love my son as always and be confident that God is not finished with him yet. What total relief it is to be able to have hope again. . . . I pray for you as you help people like myself who are experiencing "hardening of the heart"!

From all the letters shared in this book, you're probably getting the impression that it's not always easy to read all my mail every day—and you're right! There's a lot of pain in those pages. Sometimes I have to do something pretty goofy to keep from sliding back into the pit, myself. After reading one particularly poignant batch of letters, I was at the post office in La Habra in July, and the city landscapers were clipping the evergreens out front. With all the stacks of greenery lying around, the smell was pungent with the wonderful scent of CHRISTMAS!

That was all it took to give my spirits a boost. But of course I'm never satisfied until I can *share* my joy, so I quickly started looking around for my next "victim."

The doors to the post office only open outward, and I usually have my arms jam-packed with envelopes and packages, so I have to wait until some kind soul comes along to pull the door open for me. I didn't have to wait long that day. A kindly old gent came along and opened the door. I smiled and said merrily, "Doesn't it smell just like CHRISTMAS around here?"

He sort of halfway smiled in a distracted way, probably thinking it was pretty strange for someone to be talking about Christmas in July. He headed for a postal clerk, and I headed for the mail drop. Somehow we ended up going out of the post office at the same time. The somber-faced man was right behind me, and I'm not sure what came over me, but I reached down and picked off a tiny piece of the evergreen trimmings and put it in my mouth. Then I turned to him with the greenery hanging out of teeth and said, "You know, it even TASTES like Christmas around here!"

The startled look on his face was worth a million dollars to me. I laughed all the way home, remembering his flabbergasted expression and savoring that smell and taste that no one else, unless they are completely crazy like us fractured mothers are, would even notice!

Peelings from the Ceiling

Imponderables from the Game of Life:

- Why are there *interstate* highways in Hawaii?
- If you tied jellied toast to the back of a cat and dropped the cat from the roof, would the toast land jelly-side down or would the cat land on its feet?
- Why do we drive on *parkways* and park on *driveways*?

How to Know When You're Headed for Recovery

Thinking of that flabbergasted man reminds me of a story about a fellow who was riding a crowded subway train on his way home from work. He was prone to motion sickness to begin with, and he had eaten a big lunch and had worked all afternoon with an upset stomach. He wedged himself into the subway car, the last person able to get on, and the door automatically closed.

He wobbled there in the doorway of the train as the signs in the subway tunnel seemed to flash by his nose at ninety miles an hour. The longer he stood there, lurching and wobbling in the speeding train, the sicker he got.

Finally the train screeched to a stop, but unfortunately it wasn't the sick man's stop. Several people were crowded onto the platform, waiting to get on. The train stopped, the doors automatically opened, and suddenly OUT CAME THE MAN'S LUNCH—all over the guy standing in front of the crowd waiting to get on the train! The poor man waiting on the platform was so stunned, he just stood there in shocked outrage—along with all the others in the horrified little group.

Then, before anyone could move, the doors shut, the train went on, and the poor fellow found himself still standing on the platform, covered with another man's lunch. He turned to the guy behind him and said, "WHY ME?"

This is a perfect illustration of the WRONG attitude for responding to life's trials. Instead of asking, "WHY ME? WHY THIS? WHY NOW?" the apostle James reminds us that trials are inevitable and we should consider them "pure joy" because the testing of our faith "develops perseverance."[3]

Certainly, it would take quite a bit of perseverance and a really STRONG dose of cheerfulness to consider it "pure joy" when someone's lunch lands on you (mothers probably have more experience in this than fathers). But it *is* possible to respond this way if you've inoculated yourself with a strong sense of humor—and if you give yourself some time to think about it.

We all have tragedies in our lives when we flail out at God and ask, "WHY DID YOU LET THIS TERRIBLE THING HAPPEN TO ME?" At that point we need to turn things around and say, "WHATEVER, LORD!" then look for the cloud's silver lining instead of the tornado swirling in its dark midst.

We know that whatever God sends into our lives has first passed through His filter; NOTHING comes into the life of a Christian that God doesn't know about. Believing that, we can relax and know that God will be with us during the trials ahead.

When "WHATEVER, LORD!" replaces "WHY ME?" you know you are on the way to growing through your pain. An EXIT sign appears, even though it may be far off in the distance, and you start believing your "furnace experience" will eventually end.

In time you can even look back and see how God's promise in Romans 8:28 worked for good in your life.

One way to handle stress:
Lie on your back to eat celery, using your navel as a salt dipper.

Stepping Out in Style
Somewhere I read that for every single thing that goes wrong in our lives, we have fifty to one hundred blessings. What we need to do is learn to identify those blessings and spend more time counting—and being thankful for them!

Instead of wearing the galoshes of gloom we need to wrap ourselves in the "garment of praise" described in Isaiah 61:3.

This garment looks good on all occasions, and best of all it's ONE SIZE FITS ALL! It will never get too tight or too baggy. It doesn't hang crooked, and it won't hike up in the back. It is floor-length and covers all defects of the figure. It can lift the heaviest spirit, and it rests on our shoulders like a mantle to warm us with God's special love. No matter what your hair color (or whether you even *have* hair), God promises that the garment of praise will look good on us.

Looking for Joy and Learning to Laugh Again

I still don't know the answer to all the "whys" that have churned up my life, but I no longer NEED to know. Instead of questioning God, I've learned to search for ways God has used these experiences for good—to fine-tune us in our spiritual growth.

For example,as Bill and I began to recover from Steven's death, we started contacting the parents of those whose names we saw listed as casualties of the Vietnam War. We did our best to share with them the comfort of God's Word. From that beginning, Spatula Ministries was born. Its name came during a gathering of crisis-hot-line supporters, when I was asked what I needed to carry out my work. I replied, "About twenty spatulas to scrape parents off the ceiling."

Larry's announcement ushered us into a new world of pain, and we soon expanded the ministry to seek out the Christian parents of other homosexuals. Our goal has always been to help parents learn to love their children *unconditionally*, as Christ loves us.

These "good things" that have come from our family's problems don't erase the pain, but they do dilute it for us. And the boomerang joy that has come from our reaching out to others has helped us laugh again. We love getting letters like these:

> I've been practicing your joyful attitude lately, and it has been really fun. For instance, my friend and I were both pretty grouchy as we were driving

to one of our job sites. I stopped the car in front of a field where a pretty horse was grazing and said, "Let's find some joy. Watch me call this horse over to the fence."

My friend said, "Girl, that horse ain't gonna come to you."

Well, I gave it my old horse call (Cooda! Cooda!) and that horse came right to me like we were old buddies. My friend got a good laugh, and the horse got a good petting, and I found joy from the both of them. It works!

ⓖ ⓖ ⓖ

As a testimony to God's grace, He gave me many funny incidents to help me survive—like the time I found my husband and my children happily jumping on our bed together.

Learn to look for joy everywhere you go. When your many troubles are giving you a giant headache remember that the iron crown of suffering precedes the GOLDEN crown of glory—that's what we'll wear on that glorious day when we'll be in heaven jumping for joy with our heavenly Father!

Peelings from the Ceiling

Just when I nearly had the answer, I forgot the question!
Ashleigh Brilliant
Pot-shot #216, © 1971

As I read my mail each day, I wish more hurting parents could find some joy to ease their pain. I sympathize with these parents, because I've been where they are. And as I read their letters, I can't help but think:

IF YOU HAVE THE SAME KIND OF PROBLEMS I HAVE . . .
PLEASE SEEK HELP IMMEDIATELY!
Ashleigh Brilliant
Pot-shot # 3392, © 1985

Give your problems to Jesus, and then focus on getting your priorities in order. You're going to need all your mental faculties in order to survive whatever is lying around the NEXT bend in the road, especially if you are one who practices the chronic-catastrophe attitude:

This is absolutely as bad as it can get—
Unless, of course, it gets worse!

When you find yourself caught in a web of unanswerable "whys," imagine your problems as a convoluted mass of yarn with such tangles that you could never straighten it out. Then imagine yourself dropping the tangles of your life into God's hands and LEAVING THEM THERE, knowing God alone can untangle the threads of our lives.

The Hardest Hurt to Handle
For many Christians what hurts most is wondering why God would "let" such tragedy happen to people who are trying to love and serve Him. If we were heartless thieves or killers, it might make sense—we could perhaps accept that bad things would happen to us as a fate we deserved.

But most of the parents I hear from are devoted Christians, loving nurturers who have tried their best to follow God's laws and to teach their children to live their lives with Jesus as their role model. These are folks who yearn to do God's will and to serve Him in all that they do. So when their world is suddenly blasted out from under them, the hurt is all the more devastating as they stand amidst the rubble, raise their faces heavenward, and cry, "Why, Lord? Why me? Why my kid?" And once again the answers threaten to be, *God DOESN'T love me! I've messed up. I'm a failure, a disappointment to God.*

If you find yourself drowning in these feelings, here are some steps you can take to endure your survival:

First, recognize what's happening. You're packing your bags for one of those futile, never-ending guilt trips into La-La Land. Keep this up, and you'll soon find yourself once again tottering down the road toward the Home for the Bewildered! Stop condemning yourself and focus instead on God's love for you.

Stop asking *Why?* and instead hold fast to God's promises. After the terrible bombing of the federal building in Oklahoma City last year, Billy Graham told the hurting families gathered for a memorial service, "I've been asked why God allows it. I don't know. I can't give a direct answer. I have to confess I never fully understand. I have to accept by faith that God is a God of mercy and love and compassion even in the midst of suffering."[4]

I love the reminder another preacher offered: "The worst kind of blasphemy is to think that God is behind all your hurt and pain. . . . God is not the author of the confusion in your life. Neither are you." Instead, turn to the heavenly Father as our great Comforter in time of sorrow. Jesus promised, "Come to me, all you who are weary and burdened, and I will give you rest."[5]

Second, don't be afraid to cry and to plead for God to help you. When you hurt, go somewhere where you can pour out your feelings. Maybe it's your bathroom or your bedroom or your closet; for me, it was the nearest dump! Don't hold back. Let go and *ventilate!*

Remember that when God created you, He *gave* you your emotions. He *gave* you tears to help drain off the abscess of pain that's broken your heart. And when you cry, remember that you're in good company. After all, Jesus wept, too, when His heart was broken.[6]

I read an essay that shared a person's reaction when he was informed he had a terminal cancer. He said, "The first thing you do . . . is cry until there are no more tears left. Then you begin to move closer to Jesus until you know His arms are holding you tight."

After Larry disappeared into the gay lifestyle, I did a lot of crying. As soon as Bill left for work each morning and I was alone in the house, I would lie on my bed and sob loudly, moaning the most heartbreaking cries imaginable. It was noisy—but it worked. Each day when I finally finished sobbing, I felt cleansed. My heart still felt squashed, but for one more day I knew I could survive.

Now I recommend this "technique" to folks whose grief is still fresh—and that includes men as well as women. I've read that some psychologists even suggest that grieving people schedule a sobbing time each day to help release their grief.

The best place for me to do this was lying on my bed and just letting the tears flow. But if you're worried about being overheard, you may want to do your sobbing in the shower. Or turn on the vacuum cleaner or the radio to drown out your wailing. The important thing is to let yourself go. Release your grief. Cry long and loud, and feel the relief it brings.

Some grief-stricken parents worry that if they ever start this kind of sobbing they won't be able to stop, but that's not true. Eventually the tears *will* end. And when you realize what a tremendous release sobbing is, and when you remember that *all* your feelings are acceptable to God—in fact it was God who *gave* you the ability to be a feeling, caring person—then you can focus on using your tears for restoration.

Third, tell yourself again and again that THIS TOO SHALL PASS! You WILL survive. Remember that you are a child of God, and He has "plans to prosper you and not to harm you, plans to give you hope and a future."[7] He has promised to be with you always, no matter what kind of cesspool you find yourself mired in. He has promised:

> When you pass through the waters,
>   I will be with you;
> and when you pass through the rivers,
>   they will not sweep over you.
> When you walk through the fire,
>   you will not be burned;
>   the flames will not set you ablaze.[8]

It may be hard to believe that promise at first. Sometimes you have to work at it. Go to a quiet place, close your eyes, and picture yourself passing through the roaring river, with Jesus at your side, and making it safely to the other shore. See yourself standing there in King Nebuchadnezzar's fiery furnace with Shadrach, Meshach, Abednego—and Jesus!—and hear the incredulous shouts of the king and his soldiers as they see you "walking around in the fire, unbound and unharmed."[9]

Pain IS inevitable. We can't prevent it, and sometimes we can't stop it once it's started. But we can CHOOSE not to be miserable. Invite Jesus to come into your fiery furnace with you, and He will place His loving hands under you and lift you up into his strong arms of protection. *Then, like the psalmist, you will be able to say:*

> I will exalt you, O LORD,
>> for you lifted me out of the depths
>> and did not let my enemies gloat over me.
> O LORD my God, I called to you for help
>> and you healed me.
> O LORD, you brought me up from the grave;
>> you spared me from going down into the pit. . . .
> Weeping may remain for a night,
>> but rejoicing comes in the morning. . . .
> You turned my wailing into dancing;
>> you removed my sackcloth and clothed me with joy.[10]

Hang in there!

Clinging to Jesus

When you find yourself sliding toward the end of the rope, tie a KNOT and hang on. And do you know what that knot at the end of the rope is? IT IS HOPE, and our hope is JESUS!

If we say a situation is hopeless, we are slamming the door in the face of God. Instead, we have to be like the little boy who stood so long at the top of the escalator, watching intently, until someone asked him what he was doing. He patiently replied, "I stuck my chewing gum on that black hand rail, and I'm waiting for it to come back!"

Like the little boy, we must believe that our happiness WILL come back. The misery WILL end, and our joy will return to us.

Learning to Cope While We Hold on to Hope

Instilling hope is part of the goal of Spatula Ministries, but while we hold on to HOPE, we still have to COPE, and that may take all the skills we possess. One mother wrote that she managed to cope by enjoying pleasant times with her homosexual son and not constantly straining for some sign of change. She shared this piece of advice:

> RELAX, AND ENJOY YOUR TIME TOGETHER—
> NO MATTER HOW HARD IT IS!

Loving our wayward children the way God loves us means loving them UNCONDITIONALLY and accepting that only God can bring about any change in them. For many parents, that means changing their attitude. The fact is, grief changes all of us. We come out of any kind of tragedy as different persons than we were before. We can come out stronger and more understanding of the problems of others, or we can come out caustic and cynical. Frankly, it's probably easier to come out bitter! But that's surely not the best. And there's help for us, if we only ask. Remember these empowering promises:

I can do all things
through Christ who strengthens me.[11]

My help comes from the LORD,
the Maker of
heaven and earth.[12]

Understanding That We Don't Have to Understand

James Dobson, in his book, *Life on the Edge*, said, "If you believe God is obligated to explain Himself to us, you ought to examine the Scripture. . . . [It] tells us we lack the capacity to grasp God's infinite mind or the way He intervenes in our lives. How arrogant of us to think otherwise! Trying to analyze His omnipotence is like an amoeba attempting to comprehend the behavior of man."[13]

To illustrate his point he directs us to Scriptures such as these:

"It is the glory of God to conceal a matter."[14]

"The secret things belong to the LORD our God."[15]

"As you do not know the path of the wind, or how the body is formed in a mother's womb, so you cannot understand the work of God, the Maker of all things."[16]

"'For my thoughts are not your thoughts, neither are your ways my ways,' declares the LORD. 'As the heavens are higher than the earth, so are my ways higher than your ways and my thoughts than your thoughts.'"[17]

Dr. Dobson explains, "What this means . . . is that many of our questions—especially those that begin with the word *why*—will have to remain unanswered for the time being."

Instead of looking for answers to the unanswerable questions, look for joy in the life you've been given and:

Let yourself be glad you're alive.
Have genuine happiness despite your condition.
Enjoy laughter.
It's available everywhere once you start looking
for it.[18]

"You've got us baffled, Mr. Messiter. The strings of your heart do go zing, but we can't seem to find out why."

Reprinted with permission from *Stitches* by John Cocker, M.D., published by Stoddart Publishing Co., Ltd., Toronto. This cartoon is licensed by Punch Publications, U.K.

God's Medicine

As Henry Ward Beecher said, "Mirth is God's medicine,"[19] and surely NOTHING is as potent as a prescription written by God Himself! I love hearing from people who have found how well "God's medicine" works. They've discovered ways to enjoy life despite the tragedies it brings.

After twelve years of being HIV positive, my brother gathered with the rest of my family for Christmas. We felt blessed and joyful. Just being together for another year was an occasion for rejoicing. Since first learning of my brother's illness, my son was also diagnosed with HIV; we lost him three years ago.

I've learned to squeeze each drop of joy from life and to appreciate all that's good. I have learned to

live just one day at a time. . . . And I've learned
that the more we share the more open others
become about these struggles they couldn't share
with anyone else.

This dear woman has learned what Scripture tells us again
and again: A cheerful attitude is SO important. Proverbs
teaches:

Being cheerful keeps you healthy. It is slow death
to be gloomy all the time.[20]

and,

When a woman is gloomy, everything seems to go
wrong; when she is cheerful, everything seems
right![21]

Dear Barbara,
    I have practiced enough for the Rapture. Would
you please call God on your hot line and tell Him
we are ready?

For a cheap diagnosis of depression, take the
Tabloid Depression Test: Walk through a grocery
store's checkout lane and read the headlines of the
tabloids. If you can do this without cracking a
smile, chances are you are SERIOUSLY
DEPRESSED! Here's a sample test:

- Bolt of Lightning Turns Toilet into Electric Chair
- Nearsighted Hubby Scared to Death by Wife's Wig—Thought It Was a Rat!
- Preacher Goes Nuts and Drowns Woman During River Baptism
- Dead Man's Heart Started with Jumper Cables—Quick-Thinking Mechanic Brings Victim Back to Life[22]

Overheard at the gym: "My husband doesn't need a physical fitness program. He gets plenty of exercise by jumping to conclusions, flying off the handle, running down my mother, flogging the kids, knifing friends in the back, dodging responsibility, and pushing his luck!"[23]

Actual letters of inquiry and complaint sent to newspaper consumer-assistance Action columns:

- "Three months after buying a couch, the place where I sit developed an indentation."
- "I bought a recliner. It has a flaw on the toot rest."
- "Is it possible when I die to have the body legally declared dead?"
- "Do roaches live inside sewer pipes with the sewage or do they just hang around the pipes underground?"
- "I've had two accidents, both with uninsured motorists, and those parties have not been

arrested. There is some silly nonsense going on about it being my fault. That's not the point!"

- "The directions on my hair conditioner say to squeeze excess water from hair and shake well before using, but it gives me a headache to shake my head that hard."

- "How many square feet are there in a lot?"

- "The doctor said I should get rid of three moles on my back. I can't even see them, let alone reach them to remove them!"

- "Where can I get information on becoming a nuclear power plant operator?"

- "Do any of the mortuaries around here have cremation? If so, can you manage to get it before you die to make sure you have it?"

- "I'm enclosing colored pictures of my hernia and I'd like you to tell me what kind of bandages I should get."

- "Once a week I bowl with the girls. Do I burn up enough calories to eat a sundae afterwards?"[24]

The secret of perpetual youth:
Lie about your age.[25]

The mind is like a television: When it goes blank, it's a good idea to turn off the sound.[26]

Most people have minds like concrete:
mixed up or permanently set.[27]

We need four hugs a day for survival.
We need eight hugs a day for maintenance.
We need twelve hugs a day for growth.[28]

Inside some of us is a thin person struggling to
get out . . . but she can usually be sedated with a
few pieces of chocolate cake.

A little girl's essay on parents:
*The trouble with parents is that they are so old when
we get them, it's hard to change their habits.*

There is a right time for everything; . . .
A time to cry;
A time to laugh. . . .[29]

6

All Stressed Up
and No Place to Go!

How to be miserable in a world full of joy.

When Bill and I started Spatula Ministries several years ago, we worked with hurting parents who were coping with losing their child in death or with a child in the homosexual lifestyle. Now when we're deluged with letters from parents who are grappling with several tragedies simultaneously, those early times when most Spatula-landers were struggling with "only" one problem seem like "the good old days"!

It's not unusual now to hear from a grief-stricken parent who is trying to remain sane while coping with one child's homosexuality, another child's drug addiction, a parent's Alzheimer's disease, and a spouse's death. "And," the letter-writer might add, "I'm having a mastectomy tomorrow"!

Here's a small sampling of the postal smorgasbord that arrives in my mail every day:

> Things have really been more than I could bear if it weren't for the Lord. My marriage has been nothing short of a nightmare. . . . Our daughter is still heavily into the gay lifestyle and has a lot of resentment toward me. Another daughter has gone into early labor and is confined to complete bed rest until the baby is born, so her children have moved

in with me. It's especially hard as I'm still having repercussions from a recent case of pneumonia. Satan has really attacked me in every way. I'm hanging on by my fingertips, but I'm right at the naked edge!

๑ ๑ ๑

My husband has been fighting cancer for two years—surgery, radiation, chemo, and it still came back. We have not heard from our daughter for three years.

๑ ๑ ๑

My son has just informed me that he is a homosexual. He has left his pregnant wife and their children after telling her he has had several relationships while they were married. I don't have to tell you the pain and sorrow we are experiencing at this time. There is concern, not only that he may have contracted AIDS but also that he may have passed it to his wife and their unborn child.

๑ ๑ ๑

Our family is devastated by the recent "coming out" of our son. Today he and some of his "friends" appeared on a television talk show—"just to have some fun," he said. I couldn't watch it. My other kids are upset and worried about going anywhere that people may speak about this show and what their brother said on it.

๑ ๑ ๑

I feel the raw pain of a mother whose child is hooked on drugs. The night I truly gave my son to God and said, "I'm not taking him back," his family's house burned to the ground. I am staying busy and praying constantly, but I HURT SO BADLY!

MAMMOGRAM TECHNICIANS ARE LIKE
MAGICIANS... THEY CAN TURN YOUR
CUPS INTO SAUCERS ! —Patsy Clairmont

Considering all the torment that children sometimes put their parents through, I think of that little cartoon that shows two parents reacting in shock as their tiny infant announces, "Have you been sleeping all night, going out after 7 P.M., eating in restaurants? Are you used to clean clothes and furniture that looks like new? I'm here to change all that!"

To the baby's announcement, some of us more experienced parents might add, "that ain't the half of it!"

Daily frustrations do wear us down, but when you add grief, loss, or failure, the burden can seem overwhelming. Our only hope is God, who promises to be "close to the brokenhearted," to hold us up and to give us courage, wisdom, and hope. Many of these parents have already learned that God always keeps His promises. When I wrote to ask permission to use one of the letters shared above, the woman promptly wrote back:

> Barb, the Lord is good and truly loves us! My husband lost his battle with cancer, but our daughter made it to the hospital just in time that he still

knew her, and we are close again. And most glorious of all, in attending a support group I met a wonderful man who had lost his wife to cancer. We truly believe God put us together and our purpose in life is to serve Him. We were married last August. Life is good, God is good, and we are blessed!

Adapted with permission from
Ashleigh Brilliant Pot-shot #3317, © 1985.

Laughing through the Storm

A strong sense of humor can help us survive any situation, but laughter doesn't make our problems *disappear*. Crises this big can't be solved by wishful thinking. Instead, we hold fast to the grace He gives us to tolerate *today*, and we trust Him to carry our burdens in His strong, loving hands—*then* we laugh!

God's grace is a miracle in itself. As one writer described it:

Grace is rebirth, transformation, hope.
It is redemption, God's clemency, a divine
response to humanity's forlorn cry, "I've fallen and
I can't get up!" . . .
Grace is always there—a hand outstretched, waiting eagerly for us to raise our eyes from our own
misery and choose life.[1]

When we accept this wonderful gift of grace, we're freed to laugh despite the earthly woes that sink us—as the writer of the following letter does. Don't be fooled; there's a lot of pain in her words, but if you read between the lines you'll see that she is inviting us to laugh along with her:

Barb, when I got your letter today I didn't even want to read it as I was so far under the carpet. When I finally decided it was time to open it and get a lift, I also realized it was time to share the highlights of the past year:

January	Fourth bout with bronchitis.
February	Five-day flu deal—passed out and bit my lip with my TMJ splint.
March	Ingrown toenails: Both big toes cut on both sides down to the nail bed with NO ANESTHESIA.
April	Wearing old shoes because of the toe pain. Fell and fractured rib—no problem.
May	Discovered foot pain had crawled up my leg—then into my last lumbar disk. Thousand dollars' worth of tests, including myelogram. Discovered pinched sciatic nerve (my *last* nerve!).

June	Discovered I'm allergic to the antidepressant I've been on for 25 years. Had to decide quickly what to do.
July	Leg, back continued to hurt. Limped along in support hose. Tried first new antidepressant—slept three weeks and walked around zombie-like.
August	Tried second antidepressant. Like drinking water.
September	Third antidepressant. Back, leg pain so bad didn't know if it worked or not.
October	Drove self to hospital in truck at 6 A.M. to undergo another myelogram. Husband couldn't get off work.
November	Hospitalized 32 hours for removal of ruptured disk and bone spur. (They don't keep you long—just charge a lot of $$$.)
November ??	Thanksgiving . . . somewhere.
December 7	Put Mama in hospital for pacemaker implant. She is 86.
December 24	Brought mother-in-law to house for two days for Christmas. Had husband's new model train running all over den, old train running all over living room. HAD CHRISTMAS IN THE BATHROOM!
January 7	Celebrated 54th birthday in bed with virus.
January 13	Friday the 13th. Had four-car wreck while going to funeral-home viewing!!! Rushed to hospital emergency room, treated and released with smashed chest, hematoma over left eye, and other injuries. NOT MY FAULT!

Otherwise, everything's great and coming up roses for spring. There is plenty more bad stuff, but the good is—-wow! wow! wow!—I AM ALIVE! I have food, clothes, shelter, and for the first time in 32 years, my husband LEFT WORK (to come to the accident scene)! There is always a bright side. It may hide, but you WILL find it!

Holidays Hurt the Most

This dear woman had a stressful year, but as you can tell, she's still looking on the bright side! And as you can also see, some of her most stressful times seemed to have occurred around the holidays. These supposed-to-be-happy times can be especially difficult for parents in pain. One mother of a gay son said her holidays were often ruined because she wanted what she could not have: "a family like other people have." Fortunately, she finally found a way to ease her pain:

> My son lives in the next block, but I have seen him only twice, and they have not been good encounters. My birthday has come and gone, Easter has come and gone, and Mother's Day has come and gone. . . .
> There are a lot of caring people in my life . . . but like David in 2 Samuel 18:33, I continued to grieve for the lost life of my son while I made my friends feel that no one was as important to me as he was.
> Then God, like Joab did to David, made me see, as you said in your book, that the sin of one person was ruining my life. That made all the difference this Mother's Day. I sent cards to all the new mothers I knew and to my young friends who care about me when it hurts. I even accepted a dinner invitation and took lilacs and candy to my hostess, a lady in her 80s, and had a great day.

This lady is climbing up out of the cesspool—and carrying a bouquet of lilacs! She is learning what many professionals recommend in grief recovery:

> To help pull yourself out of the pit,
> reach out to someone else.

Sometimes God gives us what we need in a way we didn't expect—even through suffering. As Helen Lowrie Marshall wrote in her beautiful poem:

Answered Prayer

I prayed for patience—and my prayer came true,
For many tasks were given me to do,
Demanding patience I had never known.
Each task completed found my patience grown.

I prayed for character and strength of soul,
Unmindful of the costly, bitter toll;
And there was pain to bear, and there were tears—
And character grown stronger down the years.

I prayed for inward peace of heart and mind,
A comfort I could never seem to find
Till life compelled my thoughts to turn to others,
And peace I found in service to my brothers.[2]

These beautiful lines say so clearly what is also expressed in the story about Dr. Karl Menninger, the world-famous psychiatrist. He was answering questions after giving a lecture on mental health when one person asked, "What would you advise someone to do if he felt a nervous breakdown coming on?"

Most people expected the doctor to say, "Consult a psychiatrist." Instead he said, "Lock up your house, go across the railroad tracks, find someone in need, and do something to help that person."

Many hurting parents have found a new way to share joy during the holidays by volunteering in homeless shelters, soup kitchens, or doing other volunteer activities. The important thing is not to mope around, waiting for an invitation—get out there and find someone who's even worse off than you are, or invite a lonely person to share a meal with you.

Bill and I gave ourselves a very romantic "treat" last Valentine's Day by doing something Dr. Menninger would surely approve of. We often go to a local cafe, Robert's Coffee Shop, for lunch. The owners and waitresses know us, and one day Joyce, the owner's wife, asked me how she could get some poems printed up. I told her to bring them to us and we would see if we could help.

The next day she brought about forty scraps of paper, all containing little love poems Bob, her husband, had written to her. Some were on napkins; others were on the backs of racing forms. Many were folded, worn, and tattered, but they were all precious because her husband had written them to her. He had no idea that she had saved them all, and she slipped them to us secretly so he wouldn't know what was going on.

We had them all typed up nicely on a computer, and Bill bought some bright-red, shiny folders to put the poems in. Shannon designed a clever cover sheet, and we compiled the poetry folders and waited excitedly for Valentine's Day so we could be part of Joyce's gift to Bob.

When the big day came, we went into the restaurant before the lunch crowd arrived and sat down at our regular table. Bill had this huge stack of red folders next to him. Joyce called Bob over and said we had something he might want to see. He came over wearing his white chef's hat and apron.

The waitresses all gathered around to see what was happening.

Joyce handed him one of the red folders, and he stood there shocked and amazed to see what was inside—all those poems he had written on those scraps of paper and pieces of napkins over the years. Now they were all nicely printed to share with his family. He stood there with tears in his eyes, speechless at this gift of love from Joyce, who had treasured all those loving words for all those years.

What fun that was for Bill and me! How Bill enjoyed carrying those red folders into the restaurant. What joy to see Bob's glowing face as he thought of the love Joyce showed him by treasuring those little poems over the years. It was a wonderful Valentine's Day—HER love and HIS poems—but WE were blessed by it!

Reaching Out . . . and Receiving Joy

The blessings that come from reaching out to others cannot be overestimated. I learn this anew every year around Christmas. We usually have several dozen families who have lost a loved one during the year, either from AIDS, suicide, or some other tragedy. So over the years I have started around December 14 (my birthday in case you want to send me a present!), and I set aside everything else and start telephoning the families who have experienced a loss.

Usually when I get them on the phone it takes a minute for them to connect ME with the person who writes the books and sends them newsletters. Then they call another person to the phone, and soon every phone in the house has a family member talking. They appreciate that someone cared enough to remember their loss at holiday time. Their reaction proves the truth of that adage:

> People don't care how much you know.
> They just need to know you CARE.

It is a real effort to make those calls at Christmastime, but soon the splashes of joy that boomerang back to me fill me with so much love, *my heart smiles*. I can't help but share their excitement in knowing someone really CARES about their feelings when their loss is still so fresh.

I love to remind them that GOD IS STILL IN CHARGE OF IT ALL. Then, at the end of each conversation, I ask if I can pray with them, and then I specifically pray that God will wrap His comfort blanket around them and that His peace will be with them. Somehow the idea of being wrapped in God's blanket of love reminds them they are contained in His care—and not splattered all over the ceiling.

Making these calls at Christmastime is a boomerang joy that comes back as my personal Christmas gift to myself. And I also do it because I know that traditionally, holidays are times of sharing, but they're also days of great expectations that are painful if those expectations are not met. When there's been some type of loss—whether it's caused by illness, death, estrangement, moving, or *whatever*—holidays can easily bring MORE heaviness instead of happiness for those who are already depressed.

One mother wrote:

> It's been almost a year since our daughter informed us of her lifestyle and also told us she and her lover had been together five years. Well, I've made it through the year, but I almost lost it over the holidays! I ended up in the emergency room on Thanksgiving, sick and having a case of nerves. I'm better now and learning that only through the power of prayer and the grace of God can anything change. I know I have to leave my daughter to God, but your daughter always stays in your heart.

Choose Joy!

When grief is intensified during the holidays, you may feel yourself dissolving into a whirlpool of helplessness. But remember: While pain is inevitable in this life, misery is OPTIONAL! You still have a CHOICE about how you respond to the pain that turns your world upside down. One woman who has spent several years struggling through crises said she went to bed for a year "to count the dots on the ceiling and wish my mind had an off switch so that I could stop feeling so crazy all the time." Then, she said, she came to a crucial understanding:

> Call me a slow learner if you will, but after years of counseling and a better understanding of God's grace in my life, I am finally beginning to understand what it means to take care of myself in the midst of life's cesspools. I am quicker to set realistic boundaries for myself, and I'm doing a better job of letting go of those people and situations I can't control. I never cease to be amazed at the peace and joy that floods my life these days as a result of changing what I CAN change—MY ATTITUDE! My motto is: I don't take the credit for my children's successes; neither do I take responsibility for their failures.

This lady understands what Chuck Swindoll says: "We have a choice every day regarding the attitude we will embrace for that day. We cannot change our past. We cannot change the fact that people will act in a certain way. We cannot change the inevitable. The only thing we can do is play on the one string we have, and that is our attitude."[3]

Consider these steps you can CHOOSE to take to reduce stress during the holidays:

1. Be realistic. Accept the fact that you ARE depressed.
2. Tell yourself this is NOT a permanent thing. It too will pass. It will not STAY forever.
3. Remember that anything that is going to pass can be endured for a little while.
4. Set a deadline for your depression to end and tell yourself that you will put a limit on it at that certain time. You will discard it.

This sounds like a simple system, but it *does* work. You can *decide* whether you will embrace your depression . . . or if you will choose to be happy. You can control your moods much of the time by using this simple system.

God TAKES my yesterdays,
He KEEPS my tomorrows,
He GIVES me today,
And in the miracle of it all
He PROMISES me an eternity with Him!

"Suzy's Zoo" illustration © 1992 Suzy Spafford.
Used by permission. Thanks to Alice Laing for sharing
the inspiring words accompanying this illustration.

There are also some other practical steps to reduce the stress of holiday time:

- Set your priorities. Practice saying no and eliminate any unnecessary work. Decide what's really important, and then concentrate on those few functions. Don't be afraid to change traditions.

- Be gentle with yourself. Forgive yourself for being imperfect. Spend time with people who love you, support you, and accept you as you are.

- Take time out from the hustle and bustle to be alone with God—your hope, your strength, and your promise of a brighter tomorrow.

And here are some ideas for relieving stress at any time of the year:

- *Soak in the bathtub.* More than half of those who responded to a recent survey cited taking a shower or bath as their favorite means of relaxing. "A hot, steamy bath, shower, or sauna is a relaxing reminder of warm times and warm pleasures," according to the article reporting this survey. Another bonus of a bath is that it "guarantees a reliable period of rest and privacy."[4]

- *Exercise.* Any kind of adversity creates pent-up energy. When we're all worked up about a crisis situation, we need to find a release for this adrenaline-backed power surge. One way is to explode—but usually that's not the most beneficial. A better way is to walk, run, ride a bicycle. Do whatever exercise works for you. It probably won't come as any surprise to you that my favorite exercise is . . .

- *Laughing.* "Laughing for 20 seconds . . . gives the body the kind of workout you'd get from three minutes of rigorous rowing. In the aftermath, blood pressure falls briefly . . . and a general muscular relaxation takes place," says William Fry, M.D., emeritus associate clinical professor of psychiatry at Stanford Medical School. He suggests "When you arrive home, try to walk in with a funny story instead of a complaint. And be on the lookout for the kinds of experiences that are not only funny (and relaxing) when they happen but will make good stories later."[5]

Can it be an accident that "STRESSED" is "DESSERTS" spelled backward?[6]

Holidays come equipped with stress, but keep reminding yourself that you WILL survive. When stress overwhelms me, I try to focus on the wonderful future Jesus promised us when we will live in heaven in peace with Him and there will be no more stress or pain. I love the way Lou Pinter's adaptation of the classic old Christmas poem describes that time when Jesus will come and our star-bright future in heaven will begin. As the apostle John wrote, "Behold, he cometh with clouds, and every eye shall see him."[7]

'Twas the night before Jesus came and all through the house
Not a creature was praying, not one in the house.
Their Bibles were lain on the shelf without care
In hopes that Jesus would not come there.

The children were dressing to crawl into bed,
Not once ever kneeling or bowing a head.
And Mom in her rocker with the babe on her lap
Was watching the Late Show while I took a nap.

When out of the east there arose such a clatter,
I sprang to my feet to see what was the matter.
Away to the window I flew like a flash
Tore open the shutters and threw up the sash!

When what to my wondering eyes should appear
But angels proclaiming that Jesus was here!
With a light like the sun sending forth a bright ray
I knew in a moment this must be THE DAY!

The light of His face made me cover my head
It was Jesus! Returning just like He had said.
And though I possessed worldly wisdom and wealth,
I cried when I saw Him in spite of myself.

In the Book of Life, which He held in His hand,
Was written the name of every saved man.
He spoke not a word as He searched for my name;
When He said, "It's not here," my head hung in shame.

The people whose names had been written with love
He gathered to take to His Father above.
With those who were ready He rose without sound
While all the rest were left standing around.

I fell to my knees, but it was too late;
I had waited too long and thus sealed my fate.
I stood and I cried as they rose out of sight;
Oh, if only I had been ready tonight!

In the words of this poem the meaning is clear;
The coming of Jesus is drawing near.
There's only one life, and when comes the last call
We'll find that the Bible was true after all![8]

Stress on Stage

For many years I've gone around the country speaking to
women's groups and other gatherings—"spreading my joy,"
as I like to say. I enjoy these experiences—but they do have a
tendency to raise my stress level. Sometimes when I get up to
the podium, I'm living proof of the little joke that says:

The mind is a wonderful thing. It starts working at
birth and never stops until you get up in front of
an audience!

One of my most stressful speaking times happened in
California when I was to talk to several hundred ladies during a banquet in the ballroom at a huge hotel. Everyone was
dressed elegantly, and flowers and geraniums decorated the
hotel ballroom where we were planning to have a day of joy.
The setting was lovely! The lady who was introducing me
said things like, "Barbara is so much fun and joy. We have
been so delighted by her humor and her ability to make us
laugh. This will be a joyful time for us!"

Suddenly, just as I stepped up to the podium, one of the
church workers came dashing down the aisle, waving his
arms excitedly. He yelled, "Wait! Stop! There has been a terrible tragedy. A police officer has been shot in the lobby, and
another man has been taken hostage after a police chase. We
must stop and pray for this desperate situation right now!"

Immediately all the women rose to their feet, and many
held up their outstretched hands as the church worker fer-
vently prayed about what was happening. A sense of shock
permeated the hotel ballroom.

Then the man stepped off the stage and disappeared out
the back of the auditorium.

I stood there at the podium, poised for my talk, and said to
myself, *And now I'm supposed to be FUNNY? I'm supposed to
make these people LAUGH after THAT?"*

Desperately, I asked God to show me how! Then I said
with assurance, "Well, we have put this in God's hands—
this person held hostage and this whole situation. As 1
Peter 5:7 tells us, we have cast our CARES on Jesus, and if
we really believe God has everything in His control, we
don't have to fret now. From this minute on, we are going
to know that we have done all we could. So now let's ZIP IT
UP and get on with what we were planning and EXPERI-
ENCE SOME JOY!"

The situation was immediately diffused, and eventually we were all laughing, knowing we had put it all in His hands.

That blend of laughter with prayer is a potent remedy that can ease the most stressful circumstances. It certainly helped us get through THAT situation, and the lesson we all learned as a result helped us remember:

> The only difference between a stumbling block
> and a steppingstone is the way you use it.[9]

Sometimes You Feel Like a Nut

For years, I've shared the "steppingstone" advice given to me by a wise psychologist I've called "Dr. Wells." The ideas he shared have been a lifeline to me and many others. He said:

> Your ministry seems clearly for parents of homosexuals. It encourages them to survive their losses. Even dying people die more graciously when they have hope, either for recovery or for heaven. For parents of homosexuals, their hope is for recovery from their pain, even though their chief hope may be a change of sexual orientation for their loved ones.
>
> Keep instilling hope! These parents are motivated because of their pain. They will benefit from your service. It may be wise to encourage parents of gays to unburden themselves, to stop feeling so responsible for what happened. Adolescent and adult children make decisions beyond the control of their parents. Where there is no control there is no responsibility.

I've cherished Dr. Wells's encouragement for many years. And heaven knows that *no one* needs encouragement like a hurting parent! Even a *little* affirmation can bring us the greatest results. I thought of that recently when Bill and I stayed in a lovely old bed-and-breakfast place. It was furnished with lots of antique things for us to examine and enjoy. In our room, we found a contraption made of a long wooden stick with a bellows sort of thing at one end. It was hanging beside the bed, and when I asked the hostess about it, she said it was a QUILT FLUFFER. When you slid it inside the covers and worked the "bellows," it blew puffs of air between the quilts to fluff them up, making them as light as a feather. What a difference it made to snuggle into those fluffed-up covers! It reminded me of that witticism that says:

> Circumstances are like a feather bed:
> Comfortable if you are on TOP but
> SMOTHERING if you are underneath.

Sometimes we feel like we're smothering under the weight of all our problems, then someone comes along and fluffs us up with a word of encouragement. I read another maxim somewhere that reminds us just how valuable a kind word can be:

> A word of encouragement at the right moment
> may be the turning point for a struggling life.

As the verse in Proverbs says, "Anxious hearts are very heavy, but a word of encouragement does wonders!"[10]

Sometimes it's encouraging just to be told we're not going crazy when we feel ourselves slipping over the brink into La-La Land. That's what a hospice nurse did when she reminded a grieving woman that the stress of simply trying to survive her loss might cause her to do "crazy things." The nurse told the woman she should *expect* the crazy things to happen. "You're going to do some things that aren't like you at all," she said.

Then she reminded the woman, "That's okay. After all, you're NOT yourself right now. You're hurting, and you're lost. So don't be too hard on yourself when you lose the house keys or pay the phone bill twice or put salt in your tea or forget where you parked your car. Be patient with yourself. Gradually, your upside-down world will right itself, and you'll find your life returning to almost normal."

That nurse was right. I know, because I've done a lot of crazy things—not always deliberately! I've learned firsthand that when grieving people say they're "losing their minds," they aren't kidding. For so many of us, grief sweeps through our brains like a whirlwind, wiping out all sorts of brilliant ideas, not to mention the mundane facts we need to survive everyday life. (Of course, at the time this may not seem like such a great loss because we hurt so bad we don't expect to survive anyway!)

Instead of criticizing yourself when you do something goofy, find a way to laugh about it. As someone said, if you find yourself tottering down the road to the Home for the Bewildered, you might as well enjoy the trip. And if you aren't doing crazy things, some would say this is the perfect time to *invent* some silliness to put some laughter in your life. Here are some suggestions for "living dangerously" when you're caught up in the crazies:

- Break out dancing every now and then—tap, rap, or jig. It'll help you pass the time until they come to take you away.

- Have chocolate pie for breakfast.

- Do *not* come in out of the rain.

- Pop popcorn without putting the lid on.

- Rip those tags off your new pillows!

- Order a "happy meal" at a fast-food restaurant and play with the toy.

- Tape and replay a baseball broadcast "without the express permission of Major League Baseball."

- Wear two shoes that *really* don't match.
- Brush your teeth with Cheez Whiz.

If we're going to be lost in a fog, we might as well have fun while we're there! In honor of the souls out there in Looney Tune Town, here's a collection of my favorite "mindless" funnies.

For God has not given us a spirit of fear, but of power and of love and of a sound mind.[12]

I write down everything I want to remember. That way, instead of spending a lot of time trying to remember what it is I wrote down, I spend the time looking for the paper I wrote it down on.[11]

Dear Barbara,
   I recently attended my twenty-fifth class reunion and was voted most changed. My husband says that was a compliment, but I can't accept that because I have gained seventy-five pounds since I graduated.

   Offended in Ogallala

Dear Offended,

At your twenty-fifth class reunion you wear a name tag so your classmates will remember who you are. At your fiftieth reunion, you wear one so YOU will know who you are.

Anyway, it is better to gain weight than to lose hair, as some *men* do. Actually, when men get older they don't LOSE their hair, it just goes underground and comes out their ears! And we all know why it isn't necessary for a MAN to have HIS face lifted. If he is patient, his face will rise right up through his hair!

Dear Barbara,

Lately I keep forgetting important things like names and birthdays. I AM living somewhere between menopause and large print, but is this normal?

Forgetful in Fresno

Dear Forgetful,

We all know that the reason why women over fifty don't have babies is that they would put them down someplace and then forget where they left them! This little ditty may cheer you:

My bifocals are adequate,
My dentures fit fine.
My facelift is still holding,
But I sure do miss my mind!

So just enjoy your life, even the parts of it you can't remember!

Dear Barbara,

A friend of mine who is only fifty years old tells people she is sixty because she looks GREAT for sixty but AWFUL for fifty. Should I let people know she is lying?

Peeved in Podunk

Dear Peeved,

There are a couple of Scripture verses on lies that I get twisted up sometimes . . . but I think it goes like this: A lie is an abomination to the Lord but an ever-present help in time of trouble!

Just encourage her by reminding her that some people never lose their beauty; they merely move it from their faces into their hearts.

I keep thinking I've forgotten something...

7

You Are the Answer to Several Problems I Didn't Even Know I Had Until I Met You*

If you want to make a friend, let someone do you a favor.

After several years of marriage, Barney was asked to work on a temporary assignment in Northern California. Since he would only be there a couple of months, Shannon and the two girls stayed behind in their Southern California home. It was a difficult separation as it was the first time they'd been apart for any length of time.

When Barney had been gone about two weeks, Shannon flew up with the girls for a visit. They had a fabulous time—but drama unfolded when they got back to the Los Angeles International Airport on their way home. I'll let Shannon tell you what happened next:

We had wanted to spend every minute possible with Barney, so I had booked us on the last flight to return home on Sunday night. It was almost midnight when we landed at LAX, and we'd been so excited about seeing Barney that without realizing it I had parked in the farthest lot from the main terminal. When the airport shuttle finally dropped us

---

* Ashleigh Brilliant Pot-shot #4892 © 1989.

off by the car, I started the engine, and suddenly smoke started pouring out from under the hood.

I thought, *Oh no! I'm thirty miles away from home with my little girls and it's midnight and smoke keeps billowing out of the car!*

At the parking-lot tollbooth, the attendant said, "Something's wrong with your car!" and I thought, *No kidding! You think I don't know it?* I could hardly see out the windshield!

I started praying, *Lord, please help us get home.* I told the girls, "Just pray that His angels will look over us."

As I slowly drove a few blocks from the airport parking lot, another car came alongside of me, and the driver yelled, "Turn left! There's a gas station up ahead!"

I knew I couldn't keep going—I thought the car was going to explode. So I turned left and pulled into the service station and desperately asked the man in the bullet-proof booth if he would help me, but he wouldn't even come out of his safe booth.

Getting back in the car, I wondered whatever would I do. Then, out of the corner of my eye, I saw two men coming toward me. They were about my age but dirty and ragged, looking like street people. I sat there praying, *Lord, if You've ever answered any of my prayers, please answer THIS one because I need help RIGHT NOW!*

And when I did that, suddenly I felt a great sense of peace. That's when one of the young men said, "Ma'am, pop the hood. Then you all need to get out of the car."

Somehow I listened to him. He looked under the hood and said, "You have a blown radiator hose, ma'am. Do you have anything in the trunk we could use as tape?"

I stood there, close to tears, shaking my head negatively. Then the Lord reminded me: *The first aid kit!* I had some adhesive tape in there. I got it out, and he used it to wrap around the hose real securely. Then he put some water in the radiator and asked me how far I had to go. I told him about thirty miles.

"You'll make it," he said with a kind smile. "You'll make it home."

With only ten dollars in my purse, I gave the men five of it. I told them, "I don't have much money to give you, but I'm gonna give you something far better: I'm gonna pray for you guys and ask Jesus to bless you both. Thank you so much for helping us."

By this time we were back in the car, and the two men were standing beside it. One of them closed the car door for me as I got in. The service station was surrounded by a huge parking lot—it was a long way to the fence. I bent down to put the key in the ignition, and when I looked up they were gone. *Gone!* I couldn't believe it! I had only looked down for a second, and they had been standing right there. There was no way they could have gotten to the fence that fast or jumped it to cross the street.

Those two men had simply vanished.

For He orders His angels to protect you wherever you go.
Psalm 91:11
TLB

I wondered about them all the way home. They were right about what they had said. We did make it home, and when I called Barney the next morning and told him about it, he said, "Well, I was praying for you, and I asked God to put His angels around you. I guess He did!"

Shannon has been such an "angel" in our family—and to so many others—so I think it's only fitting that she has had a few angelic encounters in her life too. And her story of the street-dwelling "angels" illustrates what so many hurting parents already know: Sometimes God's help comes to us through those from whom we least expect it!

This lesson was pointed out to me again when a mother wrote to say that after her homosexual son's death from AIDS she struggled to find someone who could help her deal with her grief. Her church friends had seemed to withdraw when they found out about her son's homosexuality and AIDS. "We felt like lepers," she said sadly. Her non-church friends had never suffered a similar loss, so while they tried to offer comfort, they couldn't really understand the depth of her pain.

To her amazement, the person who eventually helped her the most was her son's former partner, a young homosexual man whom she had refused to let come into her home while he had lived with her son. After a chance encounter, they met again to share their grief—and their memories—about her son. And in doing so, they both began to comfort each other, proving: GRIEF IS DIVIDED WHEN IT IS SHARED.

Peelings from the Ceiling

**I probably deserve the medal for loneliness . . .
But who would think of nominating me?**
Ashleigh Brilliant
Pot-shot #188, © 1970

*Now I know without a doubt
that the Lord sent his angel
and rescued me.*

© 1995 Suzy Spafford. Used by permission.

Showing Christ's Love . . . through Friendship

Friends are so vital to those who are floundering through life's cesspool. Surely they are sent to us by God to bring comfort and lead us out of the dark tunnel. I read a little story somewhere by an unidentified writer that describes so succinctly the responsibility Christians have to reach out in friendship to those who are in need. It said:

> On the street I saw a little girl cold and shivering in a thin dress, with little hope of a decent meal. I became angry and said to God: "Why did You permit this? Why don't You do something about it?"

God replied, "I certainly did do something about it. *I made you.*"

The same idea is expressed in a letter that said,

God doesn't take away our cross, but He sends other Christians to help us carry it.

To reach out to others, we can start by sharing a smile, an encouraging word, an opportunity to laugh. That's what a complete stranger did for Bill and me recently when he shared a delightful moment with a whole planeload of people as we were flying home after a speaking engagement.

Our plane had landed, and before we could unfasten our seat belts, the captain of the plane came out from the cockpit and announced that he would like the first fifty passengers off the plane to do something that would be just for FUN (no other explanation was given).

He said there would be a young lady standing at the bottom of the ramp, and each of us was to just hand her a red rose (which he would give us as we departed) and that was all—just hand it to her. We had no inkling of what was going on, but Bill and I gladly took a rose as the pilot distributed them to the first fifty passengers.

As we walked down the ramp, this darling gal, about twenty-three or so, was eagerly waiting there. We dutifully handed her our rose as we came off the plane. She look surprised after the first couple of roses were placed in her hands, and then, finally, as the fiftieth rose was given to her and her arms were brimming with beautiful red blossoms, you could see her amazement.

All of us sort of stood around, waiting to see what joyous event we had been a part of. Then the captain himself came out holding a rose and laid it among all the others she held in her arms. Suddenly a smiling young man, about twenty-five years old, dressed in a blue suit and as handsome as he could be, joyfully bounded down the ramp, bent down on his knee, and produced a diamond ring, which he slipped on her finger after a lingering kiss.

All of us who had been standing around—executives with briefcases, men and women holding carry-on luggage, tourists with shopping bags of souvenirs—suddenly were a part of this. We were all caught up in the emotion of it. There was a clapping of hands and some shouts of "Go, man, go!" and little children who didn't know what in the world it was all about were laughing and clapping. It was as if in that brief moment we all were able to brush aside the cares of the world, set the briefcases down, and CHEER as we shared the joy of this happy couple.

CALVIN and HOBBES By Bill Watterson

What a happy gift they gave us—a real splash of joy, a sparkle that has brightened my day each time I remember it. Sometimes that's all it takes to be a friend to someone else—sharing your own joy.

Pools of Blessing and Refreshment

What this young man did is what Jesus asks us to do for those who are hurting—reach out to them and share His light with them. Cry with them and laugh with them. And in doing so, we help ourselves as we live the promises of Scripture:

> He who refreshes others will himself be refreshed.[1]
>   and . . .
> Happy are those who are strong in the Lord,
>   who want above all else to follow your steps.
> When they walk through the Valley of Weeping,
>   it will become a place of springs where pools of
>   blessing and refreshment collect after rains![2]

Isn't that a wonderful picture—that by being "strong in the Lord" we can transform someone's "valley of weeping" into "a place of springs where pools of blessing and refreshment collect"!

Steppingstones Across the Cesspool

Reaching out to others doesn't mean we adopt all their problems as our own, or "take them to raise," as a farmer might say. Sometimes we can help others through the smallest—or silliest—acts of kindness. When one woman who was going through a difficult time had to miss work to have surgery, her coworkers let her know they planned to wear hats with geraniums in them in her honor while she was away.

Sometimes the simplest little kindnesses can have enormous results. I learned that last year when I was speaking to several thousand youth workers at a convention. I noticed one lady sitting in the front who looked as though she was going to pounce on me when I finished, and sure enough, when the program ended she immediately scrambled up the

ZIGGY By Tom Wilson

stairs and onto the platform. She was so excited, her story seemed to tumble out in one long sentence:

"You remember when you were here last year and you were signing books at a Christian bookstore and a young man told you his brother was dying of AIDS but his real concern was for his mom because she was just wanting to die along with her ailing son. WELL, you GAVE him your book *Stick a Geranium in Your Hat* and also a tape of your story, and he brought it home.

"I have to tell you: I AM THAT MOTHER!

"I played the tape and devoured the book and decided I had to get up and get moving . . . I had a son who was dying in the next room who wasn't right with God! It changed my life! It changed ME! I got up from my bed where I had been languishing. I was full of hope and life, and I took that book and tape to my son and together we went through it chapter by chapter and played the tape over and over and he got his life right with God, confessed his sin, and had a marvelous renewal of his spirit. And on Christmas Day he went to be with the Lord."

By the time the woman had excitedly rushed through her story, she was breathless and we were both overcome with tears and joy! God gets ALL the glory for bringing restoration to that little family, and it is such a splash of joy for me when I get to share in His special way of putting fractured lives back together!

Friends help us just by their willingness to laugh at the goofiness that unexpectedly pops into our lives to brighten the dark places. One woman wrote to describe how her friend gave her a laugh as she was recovering from cancer. Chemotherapy had caused the woman to lose her hair, so she wore a wig. Later, her friend was helping her "get back together" as she came out of the recovery room after surgery. The woman wrote:

> She put my wig on me, and when I reached up to see if it was OK, she had put it on backwards. . . .
> I said, "Marge, you've got it backwards."
> She said, "Are you sure?"
> I said, "Yes, my bangs don't curl upwards!"
> I tell everyone I'm sure glad she didn't try to put in my false teeth!

Laughter dulls the sharpest pain and flattens out the greatest stress. To share it is to give a gift of health because, as someone pointed out,

> Ulcers can't grow
> while you're laughing.[3]

And neither, I might add, can grief.

What Can We Do?

Sometimes it's hard to know exactly WHAT to do to help someone. Here are some ideas shared by Spatula-landers who have been on both sides of this situation—the hurting side and the helping side.

- Don't say, "If there is anything I can do, just let me know." Offer specific ways of helping and show that you're ready to put your words into action: Ask if you can go to the bank or the post office, answer the phone, pick up dry cleaning, meet relatives arriving at the airport, or babysit the poodle.

- Don't bring desserts; that's what everyone else will bring. Bring foods that can be eaten easily by a crowd with little preparation: sandwiches, bags of cleaned veggies and a cup of dip, a case of assorted soft drinks, a plate of sliced cheeses, a pot of chili and a stack of disposable bowls. Or bring a casserole in a disposable pan to stick in the freezer for after the crowd leaves and the hurting parents are too miserable to think of cooking.

- BE THERE! Show up. Knock on the door, offer a hug. Sit down and visit for a few minutes. Hurting people often need to talk. LISTEN! Don't worry about making profound, memorable answers. Just listen. Don't launch into a litany of the misfortunes that have plagued your family or other friends. They're the ones whose hearts are broken now; that's all they can deal with.

- Be alert to signals that it's time to leave. If the pastor comes, if a loved one from out of town finally arrives, if another friend drops by to visit, take your cue and say good-bye. Come back later when the crowd has left and the lonely finality of the parents' anguish is settling in. That's when they need your visit—and all the previous ideas—the most.

- Invite the parents to do things with you—go to church, attend a play, visit a park, come for coffee. And if they decline, ask them again another time—and keep asking (without making a pest of yourself) until they're ready to venture out again.

- Attend the funeral. Don't assume the hurting people know how you feel about them and their loved one. As someone said, "Showing up is the only thing that counts."

Start with Prayer

When we start thinking of things we can do, we begin with prayer—surely one of the most important ways we can help. I love the verse that says:

> I will deliver those for whom you intercede, not because of their innocence but by the cleanliness of your hands.[4]

That verse can apply to so many situations, especially to the prodigals—and their weary parents. And of course our "cleanliness" comes from being washed in the blood of Jesus, rinsed in His grace, soaked in His mercy, and brightened by His love. When we pray in His name, God has promised to listen. All we have to do is . . . DO IT! As a reminder to pray for those in need of help, a nurse sent me this "handy prayer." Now whenever I happen to glance at hands, I'm reminded to pray.

THE THUMB, nearest you, reminds you to pray for those people who are closest and dearest to you.

THE FOREFINGER is used for pointing. It represents all who teach us and those to whom we are responsible.

THE MIDDLE FINGER is the tallest, so it stands for important people and leaders in all walks of life.

THE FOURTH FINGER, or ring finger, is the weakest of all, so it symbolizes the sick or those in trouble.

THE LITTLE FINGER is the smallest, so it stands for persons who are small and seemingly of less importance. (The nurse who sent me this prayer said she considered the little finger as herself!)

I read somewhere that "Prayer is a little bit like eating salted peanuts; the more you do it, the more you want to do it."[5]

SMILE AWHILE By Roy Mathison

"Thanks for confiding in me. By the way, you've got the wrong number."

"Smile Awhile" used by permission of Roy Mathison.

In addition to praying for those who are wrestling with grief, probably the next most important thing we can do is LISTEN to them! So many parents write to me saying they have no one to talk to . . .

Dear Spatula Ministries,
    The main reason I am writing is to find out if there is someone (a mother who has been through it) in our area that I could talk to. . . .

👁 👁 👁

Dear Barbara,
　　I need help, I need prayers . . . lots of prayers for myself and my son. Do you know of someone. . . ?

⑥ ⑥ ⑥

Dear Barbara,
　　This month's newsletter carried a statement that said, "A friend is one who strengthens you with prayers, blesses you with love, and encourages you with hope." . . . I do not have a friend like that. . . . I have no one here to talk to about anything, let alone THIS!

Maybe the best thing we can do is just offer a place of refuge and a listening ear for our fractured friends.

Starting a Support Group

When I read letters like these (as I do every day!) I wish I could be in a dozen places at once so I could reach out to these hurting parents who feel so isolated. I try to call as many as I can, but I know it would be even better if they had even one understanding friend who could share time with them on a one-to-one basis.

That's why support groups can be such a blessing to hurting parents. They give you ideas for coping with the challenges you're struggling to overcome, and best of all, you've earned your credentials to share what you've learned with others.

**In so much as anyone
pushes you nearer to God,
he or she is your friend.**

I have received dozens of requests from parents who ask how they can start a support group in their area. Recently my friend Kathleen Bremner, director of the Spatula II group in San Diego, put together some excellent guidelines that summarize all the things we've learned. She begins her article with a quote from Dan Allender, author of *Bold Love:* "We must discover God's power to care about others when our heart is breaking; we must find God's love to reach out to lost people even though our pain continues." I'm grateful to Kathleen for her permission to reprint the following summary of these guidelines:

To begin, you must be willing, honest, and courageous enough to open your own life and your family to public knowledge. Your heart must be pure; this should not be used as an opportunity to condemn or retaliate. The group leader should be someone who cares deeply about a loved one and has known the pain in discovering the loved one is homosexual.

Go to your pastor and share what God has placed in your heart. Ask if you could give your own testimony during a special presentation to the church. When this is agreed, choose the day, time, and location of your support group meeting.

(Barb's suggestion: Plan to hold your first meetings in your home; invite a few people for coffee and keep the gathering small. I usually recommend that meetings not be held in your church because some parents worry that they will be recognized there. When the size of the group outgrows your home, consider moving to a neutral location, such as a YMCA. Eventually, when the members of the group seem comfortable with each other, you might consider the church as the best meeting site.)

Select a name for your ministry, prepare and have printed a flyer/brochure with information and pertinent facts in time to hand it out during your presentation.

Promote the program in your local newspaper and through the churches in your community as well as your own church.

Guidelines for Your Meetings

Set up the room in a small, comfortable circle, and prepare yourself for a wonderful experience as you discover through reaching out to others that your own healing will begin.

1. As people arrive, introduce yourselves by first names only. Be cheerful, outgoing, and greet people with a warm handshake—or a little hug if you feel comfortable doing so. Make people feel "at home."

2. Use only first names during your meeting, but ask people to sign their name, address, and phone number on a card you have prepared for your records. Ask if it is all right for you to send them materials or announcements of meetings.

3. It is good to open your meeting with a short prayer, but you may find that opening the meeting in a casual way by first just getting acquainted puts people more at ease. Be sensitive to the fact that some families are not used to praying out loud. Some folks may find their way to your meeting who have not been in church for many years. Be sensitive to them. Remember God works in many ways!

4. Begin by introducing yourself and by telling a little about your own situation. Explain that everyone in the room has someone who is in the same place. Turn to a person who you may have already talked to before the meeting and ask if she would like to share a little about why she has come to the meeting. If the answer is "I'm not ready yet" go on to another person. It is important that you ask—it is easier for someone to respond when asked than to initiate his or her own story. You might say, "Tell us about your loved one . . . " or "Tell us how *you* are feeling right now."

5. YOU WILL NEED TO BE A GOOD LISTENER. However, do not let someone take over your meeting

and make it impossible for anyone else to tell his or her story. This can easily happen because when you have a large group (more than eight people) the time will go quickly, and you may find that you have not given everyone an opportunity to share.

6. People need to hear from you as their leader. They need to hear how you have been helped, where you have found your strength and comfort.

7. When you have heard from everyone, encourage them to respond to each other. Interaction makes your meeting what it is supposed to be—a "support" group meeting. The exchange of ideas and backgrounds helps people recognize that their needs are the same. Comfort comes from sharing, caring, and eventually developing a strong sense of family support.

8. When you feel comfortable, close your meeting with a prayer. In the beginning it is usually better that *you* or a trusted pastor, if one is present, close the meeting in prayer.

9. Close your meeting promptly. People will often stay afterward and want to talk together, but the meeting itself should end on time.

Some Things NOT to Do

1. Do not give out people's phone numbers or addresses to anyone without their permission.

2. Do not try to solve people's problems, and do not give advice; instead, suggest options or alternatives. Ask the group for suggestions.

Some Things to Do

1. Trust in God to guide your meeting. Ask God to give you the wisdom, compassion, and sensitivity to help people who are hurting so desperately. To some people,

discovering their child is homosexual is like death—to then learn that the child has AIDS is another severe blow. The human spirit will rise to comfort and will be filled with compassion as the healing process begins in the actual physical outreach to a loved one.

2. Encourage people to put their trust in our heavenly Father. God can change people. WE cannot. We can only change ourselves and the way we react to situations. We are not responsible for things we cannot control.

3. Learn to share laughter and amusing stories. You will learn that there is healing in laughter, and you do not want your meeting to end up as a miserable "pity party." It is most important for people to hear that there *is* life even after discovering their child is gay.

4. Remember grief is a PROCESS, and each one must be allowed to go through this process. You are there to be a support and a guide to the family to find their peace and strength in the mercy and love of Jesus Christ. People must learn that there has to come a time when they set aside their sorrow and begin to love themselves and let that love shine in the world.

5. You will have families who have just learned their loved one is HIV positive or has AIDS. You should be well informed on HIV and AIDS, but you should also have a trusted professional to refer people to for clinical and medical questions. Your purpose is to be there for comfort, spiritual help, and support. Leave medical questions to the authorities.

Kathleen closes her guidelines by saying,

Your support group should be a ministry of restoration and hope. Where there has been a break in relations among family members, your purpose should be to help restore this relationship. However, you are not God!

Only through prayer, faith, and trusting in the power of the Lord Jesus Christ will reconciliation occur. You can only direct a person to seek God's Word and His healing power to make changes in his or her life or in any loved one. With your faith and the love of God, you will be a blessing and a witness to the wonderful miracles God does promise. Be yourself. You are unique. God has given you a gift—a gift of caring about other people. Now, untie the gift!

To Kathleen's list I would add one more piece of advice for the group leader: Assure parents they *WILL* feel better. They WILL get through this trauma. Remind them that our goal is to comfort *THEM*, not to make changes in others. With God's help, *THEY* will change. They will become more compassionate, more caring, more understanding!

Keep Things Short If They Can't Be Sweet

And to those of you who might have been fortunate enough to find a support group—or a close friend—who will listen to you, I would suggest that you not overwhelm the person or the group by reciting all the details of your whole, painful story at one time. In other words,

> Don't dump the whole load of fertilizer
> on one little strawberry plant!

Having said that, you can probably guess which of Kathleen's guidelines I like best: The one about laughter! I love to laugh. I agree with the nurse who said, "I think the eleventh commandment should have been: Laugh and be merry."[6]

To reinforce that "commandment" before we leave the topic of support groups, I want to share another silly card I saw. It offered these zany observations:

All I Need to Know about Life
I Learned from My Support Group

- Don't trip on the first step!
- It's OK to let your inner child talk to strangers.
- You're only as sick as your secrets.
- Everyone's closet could use a little airing out.
- If you can't let go of the pain of the past, milk it for all the sympathy it's worth.
- "12 Step" is not a country-western dance craze.

- If you're not dysfunctional, you're not normal.
- Attendance is better when coffee and donuts are served.
- Independence, not co-dependence!
- It's hard to become a more loving person if you don't like people to begin with.
- Listen to your inner voice, but make sure to get a second opinion.
- Get over it, already!
- And remember, as you go through life, IT'S ALL BASICALLY YOUR PARENTS' FAULT ANYWAY.[7]

If there are no support groups in your area . . . start one! There you'll soon learn the truth of these two little gems of wisdom, sent to me by mothers who've been helped by others' thoughtfulness:

**When you help others,
you heal a little yourself.**

and . . .

**Love is a magic doorway through which any soul
may pass from selfishness to service.**

A Powerful Tool in a Powerless Situation

While support groups can be godsends to hurting parents, there's really no substitute for that one dedicated friend who loves you no matter how miserable you are and no matter how hard you are to be with! Just imagine how comforting it would be to have a friend who would listen to you pour out your feelings of being "terrified of the future," as one mother of an AIDS victim wrote. Or to listen to another mother express "fear for my son, terror for his eternal destination, and my grief for what seems lost."

What an honor—and a blessing—it would be to reach out to a friend in that way to pull that person back from the brink

of despair. If you can be a friend like this, you are a lifeline—
a tool used by God to bring His love to an otherwise hopeless
situation.

But God's "tool" is also blessed by the kindnesses bestowed
because:

> A kindness done is never lost.
> It may take awhile,
> but like a suitcase on a luggage carousel,
> it will return again.[8]

The Blessing of Friends

I'm especially thankful that I know *spontaneous* friends,
people like the woman Erma Bombeck described in a column
as her "seize-the-moment" friend who is always willing to
drop everything to share a bit of her time with someone else.

In contrast, Erma recounted the numerous times she had
called her own sister and asked, "How about going to lunch
in a half hour?"

Her sister would say, "I can't. I have clothes on the line."
"My hair is dirty." "I wish I had known yesterday." "I had a
late breakfast." "It looks like rain."

Erma wrote, "She died a few years ago. We never did have
lunch together."

Her sister wasted all those opportunities for sharing,
laughing, and loving.

And there's another kind of friend I'm grateful for: the one
who will allow *me* to be helpful.

Erma Bombeck asked in her column, "How often have
your kids dropped in to talk and then sat silently while you
watched *Jeopardy* on television?" When you're stuck in the
cesspool and someone invites you to chat awhile, share a
lunch, or go for a walk, it's too easy to say, "My hair is dirty"
or "It looks like rain" and then crawl back in your cocoon,
turn on *Jeopardy,* and mindlessly grieve some more.

When this happens to you, imagine not your friend but
Jesus standing before you, His hand outstretched. Imagine

Him saying to you what He said to the man who had lain beside the pool at Bethesda for thirty-eight years, waiting for someone to help him into the healing pool when the angel stirred the waters. Jesus said, "Do you WANT to get well?"[9]

If, like the man at Bethesda, you answer a friend's offer of help by making excuses about why you can't accept, you may be refusing a gift sent by God.

Such refusals remind me of the man whose farm was located on the banks of a flood-swollen river. As the water rose, a neighbor drove up in a Jeep, urging him to leave before the farm was flooded.

"Oh no," said the man confidently, "God will save me."

The water rose higher, and the man was forced to move into the second story of the farmhouse. A police boat soon came, and the officers called for the man to hurry and get into their boat.

"Oh no, that won't be necessary," the man insisted. "God will save me."

Finally the house was completely engulfed in water, and a Coast Guard helicopter swooped in to rescue the man, now perched on the roof. Again he refused. Just then, a huge wave of water swept over the house, and the man drowned. When he got to heaven, he stormed at the Lord, asking WHY God had let him die when his faith had been so strong.

"What do you mean?" asked the heavenly Father. "I sent a Jeep, a boat, and a helicopter—and you wouldn't budge!"

Helping Others by Letting Yourself Be Helped

If you're refusing to budge from your cesspool when a friend is inviting you to leave, you're not only denying a gift for yourself, you may also be depriving the friend of a much-needed blessing as well.

For some people, it's extremely difficult to accept help. They're afraid that by accepting assistance they will become obligated to that person; they think they'll become indebted, and they don't like owing anything to anyone! But what they don't realize is that by refusing help, they are stripping that

person of something good. So even when you'd rather stand
alone . . .

> In your grief, go limp,
> And let others carry you for a while.
> In doing so, you'll make a friend!

It's frustrating when you know all the
answers—and nobody bothers to ask you the
questions.[10]

> They might not need me—yet they might—
> I'll let my Heart be just in sight—
> A smile so small as mine might be
> Precisely their necessity.
>   Emily Dickinson[11]

The holy passion of friendship is so sweet and
steady and loyal and enduring in nature that it
will last through a whole lifetime, if not asked to
lend money.[12]

Prayer is asking for rain.
Faith is carrying an umbrella.

I wish my friends could only know
    the love my heart conceals.
My fondest wish would be for me
    each broken heart to heal.
If love was something we could buy
    the rich would live and the poor would die.
I'm so glad it's free to all
    the rich, the poor, the great and small.
Let's say a prayer every day.
    It will help someone along the way.
                  Pearl Waddell[13]

The church is supposed to be a hospital for
sinners, not a hotel for saints.[14]

Your body is like a superbly engineered luxury
automobile: If you use it wisely and maintain it
properly, it will eventually break down, most
likely in a bad neighborhood.[15]

The worthiest cause is kindness,
and it is timeless.
Charles Dickens

The best antique
is an old friend.

Let us not become weary in doing good, for at
the proper time we will reap a harvest if we do not
give up. Therefore, as we have opportunity, let us
do good to all people.[16]

8

I'd Like to Live Life in the Fast Lane, But I'm Married to a Speed Bump!

Mr. Fix-it meets his match.

Sometime back I attended a workshop on how to organize your closets. The session included information on storing, packing, and other helps on housekeeping that I appreciated—so much so that I decided to go on a real campaign to get our home streamlined for efficiency.

One hint was to get clothes sorted out as to season then to have them cleaned with each one on a separate hanger with a separate plastic cover, and then store them away for the off-season using the plastic covering as each garment's own individual storage compartment.

When I saw that the local dry cleaner was having a big special that offered to clean any garment for only one dollar with a coupon, I managed to collect several coupons from neighbors' newspapers. Then I assembled all our winter suits, dresses, jackets, etc., and took the whole armful down to the cleaners with my coupons. I asked specifically if they would put each piece on a separate hanger with a separate plastic protector.

"No problem," the woman said. So I felt I was making headway on my embarkation to get organized.

When I went to pick up the load of cleaning, the gal had done just as I had requested, and soon the whole backseat was loaded with my prized clothes, each in its own storage bag.

The phone was ringing when I pulled into the driveway, so I dashed in to get it while Bill came out to unload the car. While talking on the phone, I watched him take all the clothes in bags into the bedroom, and then, a few minutes later, he came out with this huge ball of plastic almost covering him.

"Whatever is all THAT?" I asked.

"Well," he said, "I put all your cleaning away, and I'm throwing out all those plastic covers that were on all the hangers!"

There was no way to rectify the problem. The plastic was all torn up. I couldn't even TAPE it back on the clothes. So much for all my intentions to get my closets organized! But the sad thing is, Bill really thought he was helping!

It always amazes me how two people who are totally devoted to each other can have such different perspectives on the incidents that fill their lives. I've written before about Bill's and my extremely different techniques on various matters, including how to properly eat peanut butter. (I just gouge it out happily in any old direction, and Bill likes to swirl it around artfully, making sure all edges are smoothly aligned.) He also gets hung up on having his socks match—that's *really* important to him (for some reason I can't quite understand). He finally got so frustrated with my laundry habits that he now STAPLES them together before dropping them in the hamper!

I used to think Bill was pretty EXTREME about the socks and peanut butter—until I heard of another "odd couple" with an even crazier hang-up. One wife fussed about the way her husband closed the bread bag, complaining that he put the twist-tie on BACKWARD! I guess there really are stranger people than those who want swirls of peanut butter instead of dollops!

Peelings from the Ceiling

Overheard: *When I married my Mr. Right, I didn't know his first name was ALWAYS!*

In most marriages, husbands and wives eventually adapt to each other's differences, no matter how eccentric they are. One of the things I've had to adapt to is that Bill is very frugal (TIGHT is the word!). For instance, sometime back when my publisher notified us that sales of my books had reached the one million mark, Bill said we ought to celebrate. He got in the car and disappeared for a while, and I imagined him arranging some quiet little dinner party at a fancy restaurant or even shopping for some special gift for me. *Jewelry would be nice*, I thought.

Instead he came home, smiling broadly, with *two bunches of fresh asparagus!* "I know how much you love it," he said as he dropped his gift into the kitchen sink. Hardly *my* way of celebrating!

© 1990 John McPherson. Used by permission of
John McPherson. Included in *McPherson's Marriage Album*
(Grand Rapids: Zondervan, 1991).

Another time I had an exciting phone call from a man (I'll call him Mr. Smith), inviting me to come to Vancouver, Canada, to speak for a women's seminar. He said the event was a two-day program for career women that featured a cruise to Victoria to "have tea with the queen."

Without thinking, I asked, "What queen?"

"Why, the Queen of England," he said, amazed that I didn't know. "She's coming to visit Canada next year, and we've arranged for our conference women to have tea with her."

Mr. Smith said he had read my books and felt I would be a good person to speak. I protested that our ministry is sort of unique and its goal is to help broken families, but he insisted my message was what these women needed.

Finally he asked what charge I would make for this, and I replied that I have no official "charge" but whatever honorarium is given is fine with me. I nearly fainted when Mr. Smith said if I could come to speak and go on the cruise and have tea with the queen he would pay me FIFTY THOUSAND DOLLARS!

Bill was sitting next to me and heard the whole conversation. Instead of being excited and thrilled, as I was, his immediate response was, "Ask him if that is in Canadian money or American."

I don't know why I expected anything different from my no-emotion, just-the-facts-please husband. In contrast, my darling daughter-in-law Shannon exclaimed, "Wow!" Then she added, "Well, it IS wonderful that the queen is coming . . . but I would *really* rejoice if it were THE KING!"

By the way, I couldn't accept Mr. Smith's kind invitation due to some other commitments. And besides, I'd have to learn to curtsy!

Opposites Attack

Little differences in spouses' personalities, style, and attitude can add a spark to marriages when things are going well. After all, God made each of us as a unique miracle with our own individual characteristics. But in some situations—

Grow your own dope...

Plant a man!

such as parents' opposite reactions to their child's homosexuality—spouses' differing opinions can also lead to hurt feelings—especially on the wife's part.

You can sense this in the following letter sent to me by the mother of a young man who had just told his parents he was gay—and had AIDS:

The last 12 days have been an emotional roller coaster. . . . To my husband, EVERYTHING is a spiritual problem. And can't EVERY spiritual problem be FIXED? I told him AIDS CAN'T BE FIXED. We can pray and fast *forever* and it isn't going to change the inevitable.

And then there's the issue of our son's lifestyle. If he would just change, not be gay, and not be living with his "friend," then . . . then WHAT? As I pointed out to my husband, if he did all that, he would have to move out from living with his lover and he wouldn't have any place to go. I asked my husband, "Are you willing to have him move back home with us, because that's where WE come into this equation?"

We've had some difficult conversations since the AIDS verdict came in. This is hard on a marriage, even a good marriage.

Festering Misery

Judging from my mail (and my own experience), it's often the mother who is first to learn her child is homosexual. Some of these bewildered moms try to keep the news to themselves for a while, hoping to spare their husbands from the grief the mothers already know, as these letters reflect:

My husband does not know. I don't know how he would take it. I think it would break his heart. He loves his son so much, is so proud of him, and I can't take that away from him.

I have no one I can talk to. . . . My friends have children who grew up with ours, and I cannot bear to tell any of them. I feel so isolated and alone. I desperately need to talk to someone but I don't want anyone to know! I feel so ashamed and alone. My husband and I are very close, but I do not feel I can tell him his only son is homosexual. I just can't do that.

❦ ❦ ❦

My heart is breaking, and I'm looking for help. Just out of the blue, my son called me and told me he is gay. I cannot believe what his admission has done to my life. How do you get the weight of a cement block out of your chest? How do you function normally when nothing seems normal anymore?

I live in a *very small*, naive town. I went to our library but was too embarrassed to look up any books on the subject of homosexuality. . . . I have not told my husband about this and don't feel I can. He would absolutely disown our son. I have not been able to confide in anyone. I'm constantly living in fear that someone else will find out. Our family and our community are so conservative and judgmental that I'm not sure I could survive the shame and embarrassment if this became general knowledge. . . .

❦ ❦ ❦

I broke the news to my husband that our daughter was gay after having kept it from him for several months. . . . It was really hard, and I was afraid he would have a heart attack and die or never let our daughter in the house again, but he didn't on both counts.

Through all of this I have really found out what being weak is. I had to talk to myself to even walk, saying, "left foot—right foot—left foot." The pressure was almost unbearable, the weight crushing, the defeat overwhelming. But I found out that it's OK to be that weak and not be able to pray or read the Bible. For when I was weak, He gave me strength and lifted me up.

Some women write to me for help but are afraid to receive a reply from anything labeled "Spatula Ministries." Fortunately, one understanding Spatula-lander sent me some large ELEPHANT stickers to cover our logo. That way I can mail things to these freshly hurt parents without anyone knowing it's coming from an organization identified by a weary woman splattered on a spatula! I thought the elephant was especially appropriate since I often say that when families hide their feelings about their children's homosexuality it's like trying to ignore an elephant hiding under the rug!

"WILL YOU QUIT SWEEPING THE DIRT UNDER THE RUG!!"

© 1990 John McPherson. Used by permission of John McPherson. Included in *McPherson's Marriage Album* (Grand Rapids: Zondervan, 1991).

Listening with Love

Most of the women who write to me, however, have already shared the news with their husbands, and now the wives are looking for help—while the husbands are looking the other way! They write letters like these:

I can't talk to my husband because he thinks I am obsessed with this problem.

⑥ ⑥ ⑥

There is a couple in our church who have two homosexual children. The wife is big into trying to help homosexuals. She has tried to get me involved in this because she knows about our situation. My husband does not want me to do this. It's so hard to know what to do.

⑥ ⑥ ⑥

We are not able to attend the Spatula meeting in our area. My husband is not yet ready for a group gathering. . . .
Our journey through the tunnel continues. . . .

These women are *right* to want to express their feelings, because sharing your grief is an essential step toward healing. Of all the mothers I've worked with, the ones who have come through the crisis of their child's homosexuality with the least amount of "scar tissue" are those who have had someone—a friend or loved one—to *listen* to them pour out their anxieties.

Ideally, the husband should be this listening person. But let's face it: That's usually not the case. In fact, it's rare for most wives to believe there really *are* men out there who are able to do this. But I know there are some because I have heard from several. One father of a homosexual wrote, "At least my wife and I can talk about this. In fact, we can't go to bed at the same time or we lie there for hours talking about it! If we weren't past that point in our lives, this would be an effective method of birth control!"

More often, however, the husband refuses to discuss the problem with his wife—or anyone else. So many letters come from wives who are hurt not only by their child's homosexuality but also by their husbands' refusal to talk about the situation. Many times, fathers believe the child's homosexuality is just a developmental "stage" that will simply go away if it is ignored.

My son came out of the closet in 1992, and I went in. It's so lonely here in this closet. I do not even share with my minister, and my husband feels we should just ignore it and it will go away.

P.S. We are lonely, need to be encouraged by others who feel our pain, but nowhere near ready to resign!

ⓖ ⓖ ⓖ

Even though I am a Christian, I still find myself "tied up in despair." My husband has the trite belief that this is one more stage of experiment our daughter is moving through, but unfortunately whether it is a stage or experiment, I truly believe this one doesn't have a positive ending.

Being able to share—and to listen to—a hurting heart is a special gift from God, recognizing, "Out of the abundance of the heart, the mouth speaketh."[1] It would be wonderful if we could help these dads to see the value of opening up and draining off some of their pent-up feelings. But the truth is that in most cases THAT'S NOT GOING TO HAPPEN! Men and women typically react differently to crises. Women find comfort in sharing their grief. They talk and talk and talk, and as the hurt drains out, their pain is dissipated.

Men, on the other hand, don't have the reservoir of emotions that are natural to women. And, as I often say, you can't expect much energy from an empty tank!

I advise women to find another Christian WOMAN to pour out their hearts to. If you're still in the secrecy stage following your homosexual child's announcement, find someone in your family—a sister, perhaps, who already knows the details of your family's history and who will listen nonjudgmentally. Or ask a trusted friend if she could spend some time with you. In the last chapter we talked about how another mother of a homosexual can also be an uplifting helper during this time. If you know someone, try reaching out and gently inquiring whether the two of you could talk about what's happened in your family. Remember:

Sympathy is YOUR pain in MY heart.

The important thing is to find *someone* you trust who will listen to your heart. In most cases, that person is NOT going to be your husband. Generally, when men hear bad news once, they don't want to hear it again. They don't want to talk about it; they want to go play golf or fish and FORGET about it. And they can't do that if you keep bringing it up (which is what YOU need to do!).

© 1990 John McPherson. Used by permission of John McPherson.
Included in *McPherson's Marriage Album*
(Grand Rapids: Zondervan, 1991).

We have to realize that there's a limit to men's emotional strength. We expect them to be strong and supportive in crises. But grief is the one area they cannot deal with. They

grow up believing they shouldn't express their own emotions, and yet too many wives expect their husbands to be
sponges, capable of indefinitely absorbing their loved ones'
grief. Most of the time, it's just not possible.

Marriages can get in serious trouble if a woman doesn't
understand this important difference in the way men and
women typically react to tragedy. After one young man told
his parents he was gay and HIV positive, the mother said she
"cried all the way home, pouring my heart out to God and
asking Him 'why?' and asking Him for strength to carry on."
In contrast, her husband seemed completely indifferent to
their son's plight. He told the son, "Well, you played with fire
and got burned, so you must suffer the consequences of your
actions, and there is nothing I can do about that."

Another woman wrote to describe her passionate response
when she learned their son was gay. Then she added:

> After our son told his father and me he was gay . . .
> his father stood there like a zombie. I turned to him and
> asked him if he had anything to say, and he said no.

Don't Bother Dad; He's Swimming in Denial

Sometimes after dads find out about their child's homosexuality, they tend to deny that any problem exists, no matter how glaringly it stares them in the face (in the form of
their miserable wives, who feel so isolated by their husbands' reluctance to talk about it). They're like the man who
went on a photographic safari to Africa to take pictures of
elephants. The only problem was that he didn't know what
an elephant looked like, so he returned to camp that night
totally dejected.

"What's wrong?" someone asked.

"I didn't see a single elephant," the man complained. "The
whole place is being overrun by a bunch of huge gray animals
with long snouts, big ears, and stringy tails."[2]

The problem is right there in front of you, whether or not
you recognize it for what it is. The secret to surviving is not in

THE BUCKETS By Scott Stantis

Reprinted by permission: Tribune Media Services. © 1995.

ignoring it or denying it but in learning to cope with it—*unlike* the man named George in the following "parable of denial":

George deeply resented the fact that there was such a thing as gravity and that his life was so affected by it. . . . He despised gravity and the restrictions it imposed upon him. . . . He decided he was just going to ignore its existence. "I'm not going to let this gravity thing ruin *my* life," he announced.

From that day forward George pretended gravity wasn't there. If he held a piece of china or crystal in his hand, he let go of it and ignored the fact that it fell and broke. Before long his entire set of china and crystal was destroyed. He dropped his dachshund puppy so often that it would no longer come to him when he called. . . .

Then, one day George was at working looking out the windows of his office, which was on the twelfth floor. . . . He decided he'd go for a stroll. He opened the window, stepped out, dropped 12 stories, and broke every bone in his body. . . .

The moral of this little story is that you can't change the facts by denying they exist, but you can certainly hurt yourself by trying.[3]

Of course I know I'm "preaching to the choir" because most readers of this book are women, and it's their husbands who are lost in denial and refusing to change directions.

Dear Barbara,
My husband gets us lost a lot when we drive on vacations, but he always insists he is making good time. Any suggestions for him?
Lost in Louisville

Dear Lost,
Well, honey, we know the reason why Moses wandered for forty years in the wilderness was because HE WOULDN'T STOP AND ASK FOR DIRECTIONS! But then, if you don't know where you're going, any road will take you there!

I don't want women to think there's no hope that their husbands will ever change—some men can learn to express their feelings. We see this happen sometimes in our Spatula meetings. In most cases, the men are obviously not happy to be there; they've usually come at their wives' insistence. It's very unusual for them to open up right away. But usually they will eventually begin to share a little about their feelings, and when they do, their marriages improve.

So much of my mail is full of cries for help, I'm overjoyed when a letter ends with a glimmer of hope and the hint of a silver lining:

> When our son announced his homosexuality to us . . . our first reaction was one of hurt and anger. We are born-again Christians and have raised our children in the church. I remember standing in the shower that morning crying and screaming at God, "WHY?"
>
> I have been through so much since then that I sometimes wonder if the bad things will ever end. When our son made his announcement it seemed my world came to an end. It was like suffering a death, and yet he was still here. I must confess that at times I have wished he had died. It would be easier to deal with, but I know in my heart that I wouldn't want that for anything, and I live in fear that he really will die because of AIDS.
>
> My poor husband has really suffered a lot of guilt and blame. He tends to keep everything inside. . . . He has been a source of comfort to me, and our relationship seems to be growing closer through all of this.

Despite the cesspool she found herself in, this woman realized she was LUCKY because she was able to cling to her husband. Many other women long for that kind of support. And the ones who write the most poignant letters are often the wives of ministers.

Peelings from the Ceiling

**Our love is growing,
So I don't mind watering it occasionally with a
few tears.**

AshleighBrilliant
Pot-shot #453, © 1974

When the Puzzle Piece Doesn't Fit

Men, especially those who work in areas such as medicine, mechanics, or engineering, like to deal with things that can be *fixed*. To them, something to be broken is like a jigsaw puzzle—it looks overwhelming at first, but all the pieces eventually fit together.

When parents have a kid who CAN'T or WON'T fit into the puzzle, dads are stumped. They can't handle not being able to fix something that's obviously broken.

After all, they've *always* been able to fix things—up until now. Dads think back fondly to those instructive days when the kid was little and got into trouble (for something that seems so petty now). The mom would march the little guy up to the dad and say, "I've *had* it with this one! He's *yours!*" Then the dad would mete out the spanking or whatever discipline was called for and all would be right with the world. Perhaps in his sermon he would use some of these famous parental sayings:

• You'd better change your tune pretty quick or you're outta here. I mean it. Is that understood? • Don't shake your head at me. I can't hear your head rattle. • Don't mumble. • You act as if the world owes you a living. • You've got a chip on your shoulder. • You're not going anywhere looking like that. You're crazy if you think you are. • I don't know what's wrong with you. I never saw a kid like you. I wasn't like that. • What kind of example do you think you are for your brothers and sisters? • Sit up straight. Don't slouch. • Would you like a spanking? If you would, just tell me now and we'll get this whole thing over with. • I'm your mother, and as long as you live in my house you will do as I say. • Do you think the rules don't apply to you? I'm here to tell you they do. • Are you blind? Watch what you're doing. You walk around here like you're in a daze. • Something better change and change fast. You're driving your mother to an early grave. • This is a family vacation. You're going to have fun whether YOU like it or not. • Take some responsibility. Pull your own weight. Don't expect other people to pick up after you, and don't ask me for money. • Do you think I'm made of money? Do you think I have a tree that grows money? • You'd better wake up, and I don't mean maybe. • We've given you everything we possibly could—food on the table, a roof over your head, things we never had when we were your age. • You treat us like we don't exist. • That's no excuse. If he jumped off a cliff would you jump off a cliff too? • You're grounded. • I'm not going to put up with this for another minute. You're crazy if you think I am. If you think I am, just try me. • Don't look at me that way. • You look at me when I'm talking to you. • Don't make me say this again![4]

When a child comes home and says, "Dad, I'm gay," the husband wants to take *his* turn at that magical sink where parents try to wash their hands of a child. But it doesn't exist because:

You can have an ex-wife
or an ex-husband,
but you can never have an ex-child.

There will always be a space in every father's heart that's shaped just like his child. Nothing else can fill that space. But while the heart still loves, the head must also recognize that fact of life Dr. Wells shared with me so long ago that I keep repeating to myself—and to any hurting parents I meet:

Where there's no control
there's no responsibility.

Someone sent me a statement from an unidentified article that reinforces this principle so beautifully: "As parents of a homosexual, we felt the usual guilt and wondered what we or [our son] had done wrong. But we learned our only responsibility was to accept and love our son as a child of God. We learned we are accepted by God with all our weaknesses and warts."

The woman who sent me this quote added, "I can surely do that much for my child. I can love and accept her as a child of God. And that's about *all* I can do right now, but it's a good start."

Let's face it: Some things just can't be FIXED. They can only be ENDURED. And, of course, one of my favorite ways to endure any difficult situation is to laugh at it. At a talk I gave recently, I talked about men having to endure this frustration when they're unable to fix something. Later, a friend told me a story about a couple's REAL frustration:

The husband and wife were both late for work on a Monday morning and were frantically hurrying to get dressed when the zipper on the back of the wife's dress got hopelessly stuck. She struggled to free it, but the dress was one of those slim, fitted styles, and try as she might, she just couldn't get a good enough grip on the zipper to work it loose.

She asked her husband to help, and with an exasperated

sigh, he hurried over to her, grabbed the zipper, gave it a mighty yank—and broke the tab off! The woman was livid. "You *broke* it?" she cried, squirming around to see her back in the mirror. "This is my favorite dress, and you've broken the zipper!"

Unfortunately, as the man tried to help with the zipper his wife squirmed and turned frantically, trying to get out of the dress, and the poor man got tickled. *That* didn't help matters one bit! Finally the wife gave up, jerked open a dresser drawer, pulled out a pair of scissors, and pointed them at him with a glacier-forming stare.

The husband thought at first she might be planning to attack him with the weapon, but instead she barked at him, "You'll have to cut me out of it."

He quickly snipped away the dress and the wife rushed to find something else to wear, then the two of them headed off to work in opposite directions, both in a state of frustration.

The wife was still fuming when she returned home that evening and found his car parked in the garage with a pair of familiar-looking, denim-clad legs sticking out from beneath it. When she thought of her ruined dress, she momentarily considered kicking those long legs that protruded from under the car. Then a better idea came to her. She bent down, grabbed the tab of his trousers zipper, and roughly zipped it up and down half a dozen times.

She secretly *enjoyed* hearing him bang his head on the car's axle and cry out in alarm as he reacted in shocked terror. Smiling with satisfaction, she went on into the house . . . and was ASTONISHED to see *her husband* standing in the kitchen, cooking supper.

"What are you doing in HERE?" she croaked.

"I'm cooking your favorite dinner. I thought it would be a good way to apologize," he said sweetly.

"Wh-wh-who is that out there in the garage under your car?" she managed to stutter.

"Oh, that's our new neighbor. He came over to help me work on the transmission."

Peelings from the Ceiling

First, men forget names.
Then they forget faces.
Then they forget to pull their zipper up.
And then they forget to pull their zipper down![5]

Warm Yourself in the Light at the End of the Tunnel

If you're like many parents, you would gladly submit to being "cut out" of your problem situation—if only that would fix things. Instead you need to find someone who is willing to GENTLY peel you off the ceiling. Turn to the Lord, "take a new grip with your tired hands, stand firm on your shaky legs"[6] . . . and laugh!

Don't keep yourself isolated from your friends and family members. The advice I often share with parents is:

OPENNESS IS TO WHOLENESS
AS SICKNESS IS TO SECRETS!

The isolation is what sinks parents—especially mothers—the most, but we don't have to suffer alone. First, we must keep in mind that growing hurts but suffering does produce strength in our character. I think of this when I remember my friend's forty-six-year-old son who has multiple sclerosis. Part of his treatment is to be STUNG by honey bees! During the last year he has endured six thousand stings!

But the suffering caused by the stings is slowly helping his overall condition improve. As his mother says, "He won't quit the stings, and I feel certain they are doing quite a bit of good."

We should look at the inevitable pain that fills our lives the way this brave young man considered the bee stings: as a means of growth. This is what James urged us to do when he wrote that we should, "consider it pure joy," when we "face trials of many kinds."[7]

MOTHER GOOSE AND GRIMM By Mike Peters

Reprinted by permission: Tribune Media Services. © 1995.

Lean on Jesus

Most importantly, as we go through these trials we must push back the curtain of isolation and realize we are NOT alone—EVER! When it feels as if you're so far gone that no one can understand your torment, remember God's promise to Isaiah—and to all His children in all the centuries since then:

> So do not fear, for I am with you;
>> do not be dismayed, for I am your God.
> I will strengthen you and help you;
>> I will uphold you with my righteous right hand.[8]

We need to keep repeating this promise until it totally *marinates* our spirits. One woman said she and her husband do this by keeping an assortment of uplifting "Scripture cards" of verses like Isaiah 41:10 taped to the refrigerator door. She said, "When our children share stuff we wish we didn't know, we go to our refrigerator door and read again the reminders that our boys belong to God and always have—He controls their destiny."

It gives me a chuckle to imagine these two shell-shocked parents, stumbling like zombies to the refrigerator door after being hit by yet another zinger by one of their kids. I hope one of the verses they have posted there is 2 Chronicles 15:7: "Be strong and do not lose courage, for there is reward for your work."

Men have three basic hairstyles:
Parted
Unparted
Departed

As a man ages, his hair usually turns gray.
Then it turns loose.

I don't understand YOU.
You don't understand ME.
What else do we have in common?
> Ashleigh Brilliant
> Pot-shot #208, © 1970

The rooster may crow,
But it's the hen who delivers the goods.

Wisdom doesn't necessarily come with age.
Sometimes age just shows up all by itself.[9]

No man is too big to be kind,
but many men are too little.[10]

You never realize what a happy marriage
you had until the kids move back—
and then it's too late.

How to tell your husband you love him: When
the grass grows thick and tall, mow the words "I
Love You" with the lawnmower.[11]

It's always darkest just before the dawn.
So if you're going to steal the neighbor's newspaper, that's the time to do it![12]

Sign in a building-supply store: "Custom colors
will not be mixed for husbands without express
written consent from their wives."[13]

If God seriously plans to help with my problems . . .

He has a busy day ahead of Him!

Ashleigh Brilliant
Pot-shot #3740 © 1985

Sign posted on grocery-store bulletin board:
FOR SALE:
COMPLETE SET ENCYCLOPEDIA BRITANNICA
Excellent condition. No longer needed.
Wife knows everything.

A husband is a diplomat who remembers his wife's birthday but not her age.[14]

Q: What's the big difference between government bonds and a man?
A: Bonds mature.[15]

A man who refuses to admit his mistakes can never be successful. But if he confesses and forsakes them, he gets another chance.[16]

9

No, Peggy Lee, That's NOT All There Is!

We're living in palace-preparation mode!

A few months ago a two-hour talk show I was doing in Chicago was almost over. After two hours, I had shown all my props and said everything I knew to say. As the clock ticked down to the end, I was just letting out a sigh of relief when, with just a couple of minutes to go, the talk-show host said, "And now Barbara has something encouraging to say to all you TWO MILLION people watching this program."

I looked around and then realized he meant ME. Suddenly the lights were blinding and the camera zoomed in on me and the host was smiling an enthusiastic smile and I was supposed to SAY SOMETHING ENCOURAGING! What I had been WANTING to say was, "Thank heaven it's over!" but THAT wasn't very encouraging!

I was so shocked I couldn't even think of my name, much less John 3:16. *ME? NOW? Say something to ENCOURAGE TWO MILLION PEOPLE?*

I did have ONE prop left that I hadn't used. It was a little sign someone had given me, but it hadn't been appropriate that day. Impulsively, I picked it up and held it toward the cameras:

LIFE IS HARD
AND THEN YOU DIE.

Well, the show's host looked at me as if I had lost every marble I ever had . . . so I quickly gulped another breath and explained: "Life IS hard. There is sin, AIDS, divorce, sickness . . . but then we die and get to be with Jesus." I went on and said all the things about how the future is bright for us as Christians because we're promised a wonderful heavenly home where there's no more sickness or unhappiness of any kind.

When the show was over, the phone panels lit up with calls from folks who wanted to talk to the lady "who thinks it is so wonderful to die." Not that it is, but that is the ONLY way out of here . . . unless He comes for us.

My little granddaughter says I should say, "Life is hard and then we die and *get to be in heaven*." It's like the two turkeys who were discussing their philosophy of life in mid-November. One of them said to the other, "For me, Thanksgiving is the day AFTER the holiday." That's the way it will be for us (but in reverse). Our celebration will occur AFTER we die because our final exit HERE will be our grandest entrance THERE." Remember:

> Death is not extinguishing the light . . .
> It is putting out the lamp because the dawn
> has come.

Christians *know* the answer to that song Peggy Lee used to sing so poignantly, "Is That All There Is?" Driving down the road recently, I heard another song that spells out the encouraging trust that motivates us: "When they drop these bones down in the ground, I'll be living on the other side—that's right—I'll be living, I'll be dancing, I'll be praising on the other side."[1]

Psalm 90:10 says our lives are "threescore years and ten," and soon they are gone and we "fly away."[2] We're outta here! I saw a church sign that said: INTERESTED IN GOING TO HEAVEN? APPLY HERE FOR FLIGHT TRAINING! That's us! Soon we'll be putting into practice what we've been trained to expect. I like to call this training "Rapture practice." I think we should go out in the backyard and practice for the Rapture, that time when we will meet Jesus in the air as He returns. I said this once at a meeting, and a little lady came up and asked me, "When you do your Rapture practice, do you do it on the ground or on a trampoline?"

No matter where we are when it happens, one of these days, He's gonna TOOT and we're gonna SCOOT right out of here. And I can hardly wait!

RALPH By Wayne Stayskal

"HAVING 'CALL WAITING' DOESN'T MEAN YOU HAVE TO WAIT FOR A CALL!"

Recently I was sharing that line about "toot and scoot" and a young man with a terrific sense of humor who had heard my talk before was planning to get up and blow a trumpet right when I said "toot and scoot"! I'm glad he decided not to! I wouldn't have needed a trampoline to be launched into heaven if he had!

Knowing how I love this little phrase, some people end their letters to me with witty closings that remind me of what's coming. One signed off with, "Awaiting His shout!" and another wrote, "Until He comes or I go!" One woman ended her letter by saying, "May the joybells of heaven ding-dong in your heart each day!" Don't those sign-offs remind you we are EASTER PEOPLE living in a GOOD FRIDAY WORLD?

There's a wonderful old song that says, "Lift up your heads, . . . pilgrims aweary, . . . for your redemption draws nigh." We ARE pilgrims here; we're not settlers. We are only passing through this world, so we have to learn to hold LOOSELY to all that is here because soon we will be gone. We can't take it with us, but we can surely send it on ahead!

I grew up in a house that had a plaque hanging on the dining-room wall that said, "Only one life, t'will soon be past. Only what's done for Christ will last." How true that is! During our time on earth, we're preparing for our life in heaven. That means we're living in:

PALACE-PREPARATION MODE!

In other words:

> If you are interested in the hereafter,
> remember that the HERE determines the AFTER!

I received a card with a picture of a beautiful estate on the front. Inside my friend had written, "This is the mansion I have ordered for heaven . . . and I hope yours is next to mine." I framed that picture and have it in my Joy Room where I see it every day and think of how wonderful it will be when we are living in our heavenly palaces with Jesus as our neighbor! That will be the day, as another verse says, when we're "Caught up in the clouds, . . . O blessed assurance, forever with Thee."[3]

How vital it is to keep our anticipation of heaven bubbling up in our hearts, because we have to live now in a "nasty now and now" instead of the "sweet bye and bye." As Romans 8:18 says, "The sufferings of this present time are not worthy to be compared with the glory which shall be revealed in us" (KJV). In other words, heaven's delights will far outweigh earth's difficulties! And one of those delights will be seeing that:

The blue of heaven is bigger than the clouds!

How rich we'll be in heaven to have, as the old song says, a mansion, a harp, and a crown. And best of all, we'll have Jesus! Death is nothing to be feared. Instead, as one comedian said, "Death is God's way of saying, 'Your table is ready.'" When we lose loved ones, if they know the Lord, they are not gone. They have just *gone on ahead* of us to glory.

The thing that reminds me most vividly of this hope is the memo shown on the next page. I've copied and hung it in every room of my home and even in my car so I see it everywhere I go.

One of the best ways I know to infuse you with hope is Romans 15:13: "May the God of hope fill you with all JOY and peace as you trust in him, so that you will overflow with HOPE."

And do you know what h-o-p-e stands for?

> **H**e
> **O**ffers
> **P** eace
> **E** ternal!

Here on earth, pain is inevitable, but Jesus offers us PEACE ETERNAL when we live with Him in heaven! When we're dwelling in our heavenly homes, we'll never have another

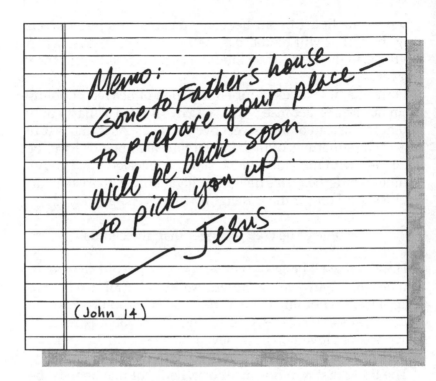

Memo:
Gone to Father's house
to prepare your place —
will be back soon
to pick you up.
—Jesus

(John 14)

worry. Can you imagine it? And just think of the other things we do on earth that we'll NEVER do in heaven:

On earth, you have driven by a beautiful hillside dotted with white markers and waving flags. But there will be no death, no cemeteries, in heaven.

Every day on earth, you flip a light switch—but you'll never do it in heaven. There'll be no darkness there (see Rev. 21:25)!

In heaven, you'll never see an old person. Sure, we're all progressing NOW through that stage between estrogen and death (or, as I like to say between *Blue Lagoon* and *Golden Pond*). Our sin wrinkles, our energy wanes, our minds go,[4] but in heaven there will be NO OLD PEOPLE! We will have new, incorruptible bodies that are glorious and imperishable. What a delight THAT will be!

On earth, as a fractured parent, you've probably shed many tears. That's one way we release our pain incurred from all the misery abounding in the world. But in heaven, God will wipe away all tears from our eyes. There will be no more sorrow or crying.[5]

On earth, you've probably taken a pill. Medications help us deal with our frailties, but there will be no drugstores in heaven because there will be no sickness, no pain. Doesn't that make you want to go home to heaven!

Do you see why my strongest message of encouragement now is "Life is hard, then you die!"? Because ahead of us we have such glory, such love, such abundance of grace, such wealth!

And while our greatest joy will come when we are eternal residents of the heavenly kingdom, Christians DO have riches on earth as well. We enjoy God's "down payment" on the wealth He promises us in eternity. If you think you've been left off the distribution list for these here-and-now riches, consider the little story about a tax assessor who came to a poor minister, trying to determine the amount of taxes the minister would have to pay.

"What property do you possess?' asked the assessor.

"I am wealthy," replied the minister.

"List your possessions, please," the assessor instructed.

"First, I have everlasting life" (John 3:16).

"Second, I have a mansion in heaven" (John 14:2).

"Third, I have a peace that passeth understanding" (Phil. 4:7).

"Fourth, I have a joy unspeakable" (1 Pet. 1:8).

"Fifth, I have divine love that never faileth" (1 Cor. 13:8).

"Sixth, I have a faithful, pious wife" (Prov. 31:10).

"Seventh, I have healthy, happy, obedient children" (Exod. 20:12).

"Eighth, I have true, loyal friends" (Prov. 18:24).

"Ninth, I have songs in the night" (Ps. 42:8).

"Tenth, I have a crown of life" (James 1:12).

"Eleventh, I have a Savior, Jesus Christ, who supplies all my need" (Phil. 4:19).

The tax assessor closed his book and said, "Truly, you are a very rich man, but your property is not subject to taxation."[6]

Truly, WE are very rich people. Sure, our hearts have been broken and our minds have been run through the wringer, but as Christians we have incredible wealth, bought for us at an unimaginable price. So how do we manage that wealth? We live joyously, sharing the good news wherever we go. I love the little verse that says, "Two eyes to look at God above, two hands to clasp in prayer, two feet to carry me to church—that's why I'M A MILLIONAIRE!"

ZIGGY By Tom Wilson

ZIGGY © 1995 ZIGGY AND FRIENDS, INC.
Distributed by UNIVERSAL PRESS SYNDICATE.

It has been said that joy is the flag you fly when the Prince of Peace resides in your heart. Our responsibility as Christians is to be contagious! Here are some suggestions for spreading your joy:

- Pray that the Holy Spirit will fill you with His joy. Happiness depends on what is happening around us, but the real JOY of the Holy Spirit comes from that deep, bubbling-up spirit inside us that gives us the ability to find joy no matter what happens to us.

- Listen to tapes and read books and articles that elevate your mood.

- Spread your joy through the mail. Write to some joy-poor friends and enclose some cartoons or humorous clippings. Share joyful news. Give others sincere praise and warm encouragement. Remember that the word *encourage* means "to fill the heart." Take some time to fill another's heart and see how that goodness will boomerang back to fill your own. There are many *squashed* hearts out there!

- Seek out some friends who are joy-givers and let them refresh your battered spirit.

- Finally, be a merry Christian! Become a joy germ, and infect everyone around you!

Do you need some encouragement? Here it is (again):

LIFE IS HARD, THEN YOU DIE . . .
AND GET TO BE IN HEAVEN!

Lift yourself out of the gloomees, warm yourself in God's love, and FOCUS ON JESUS. It's not hard. Just use your imagination.

> Think . . .
> of stepping on the shore
>   and finding it Heaven;
> of taking hold of a hand
>   and finding it God's hand;
> of breathing a new air
>   and finding it celestial air;

of feeling invigorated
    and finding it immortality;
of passing from storm and tempest
    to an unknown calm;
of waking and finding you're Home![7]

Until He toots and I scoot!

Notes

Chapter 1. **The Truth Will Make You Free . . . But First It Will Make You Miserable**

1. Jeff Rovin, *1001 Great One-Liners* (New York: Signet, 1989), 75.
2. Bill Cosby, *Fatherhood* (New York: Berkley/Doubleday, 1986), 61.
3. In his cartoon strip "Marvin," Tom Armstrong came up with this title adapted from John Gray's best-selling book, *Men Are from Mars, Women Are from Venus.*
4. Adapted line by Myrna Neims, Gainesville, Florida, published in *Laughing Matters* 9, no. 1, 27.
5. Darlyne J. Erickson, ed., *The Exchange*, Cathedral Press, Long Prairie, Minn., 4.
6. Adapted from *The Laughter Prescription*, Summer 1994, 4.
7. Adapted from *Nurses for Laughter*; submitted by a friend of Spatula Ministries.
8. Thanks to freelance writer Sherrie Weaver, Denver, Colorado, for sharing this witticism.
9. Submitted by a friend of Spatula Ministries.
10. 2 Tim. 1:7 NKJV.

Chapter 2. **I've Learned to Accept Birth and Death, But Sometimes I Worry about What Lies Between!**

1. Matt. 28:20.
2. Ps. 34:19 TLB.
3. Matt. 26:38.
4. Wiley McGhee, *Moments with God* (Puxico, Mo.: self-published, 1993).

5. Job 8:21.
6. Adapted from H. Jackson Brown Jr., *Live and Learn and Pass It On*, vol. 2 (Nashville: Rutledge Hill, 1995), 46.
7. H. Jackson Brown Jr., *Live and Learn and Pass It On*, vol. 3 (Nashville: Rutledge Hill, 1995), quoted in *Reader's Digest*, June 1995.
8. This "note" is adapted from Tim Brennan, "Simple Pleasures Are Best," *St. Petersburg Times*, 26 September 1995, 4G.
9. Carol Burnett, quoted by Patty Wooten, R.N., ed., *Heart, Humor, and Healing* (Mt. Shasta, Calif.: Commune-a-Key Publishing, 1994).
10. Charlene Ann Baumbich, *Mama Said There'd Be Days Like This, But She Never Said Just How Many* (Ann Arbor, Mich.: Servant, 1994). Used by permission.
11. See Phil. 4:8 and Rom. 12:2.
12. Thanks to Roger Shouse, Greenwood Church of Christ, Greenwood, Indiana, for sharing this story.
13. The Rev. Dale Turner, quoted in the *Seattle Times*.
14. Patty Wooten, R.N., *Heart, Humor, and Healing* (Mount Shasta, Calif.: Commune-a-Key, 1994).
15. Adapted from Brown, *Live and Learn and Pass It On*, vol. 2, 156.
16. Bill Cosby, *Time Flies* (New York: Doubleday-Bantam, 1987).
17. Corey J. Rose in *Friendly Exchange*, winter 1993.
18. Jean Van Dyke, ed., *Words to Live By: Positive Thoughts for Positive Living . . . Wit and Wisdom from Rural America* (Fort Atkinson, Wisc.: *Farming* Magazine, Inc.: 1990), 37.
19. Rom. 15:13.

Chapter 3.   Pack Your Bags—We're Going on a Guilt Trip

1. Helen Griggs, "Gone, Gone, Gone, Gone."
2. Ps. 32:1 TLB, emphasis mine.
3. Phil Kerr, "Sing and Smile and Pray."
4. Dan. 12:3, paraphrased.
5. My Joy Room, described in detail in chapter 5 of *Stick a Geranium in Your Hat and Be Happy!*, began as a Joy *Box* in which I collected jokes, clippings, gadgets, cards, and other silly items that made me laugh. Eventually my collection outgrew the biggest box, and Bill and I added a sixty-by-ten-foot Joy *Room* on to our mobile home.

6. Ps. 145:14 TLB.
7. Heb. 12:12–13 TLB.
8. Fred Allen, quoted by John and Anne Murphy in *The Laughter Prescription*, Summer 1994.
9. George Burns, *Wisdom of the 90s* (New York: Putnam's Sons, 1991).
10. "Words of Wisdom from Mr. Hooty," *Prior (Oklahoma) Herald*.
11. Caroline Schroeder, quoted in *Reminisce*, Nov./Dec. 1992.
12. Bob Phillips, *Encyclopedia of Good Clean Jokes* (Eugene, Oreg.: Harvest House, 1992), 331.
13. Ps. 71:14.

Chapter 4.   I Thought I Had a Handle on Life, But Then It Fell Off
1. Helen Keller, quoted by Wooten in *Heart, Humor, and Healing*.
2. Erma Bombeck, quoted by Wooten in *Heart, Humor, and Healing*.
3. Verdell Davis, *Riches Stored in Secret Places* (Dallas: Word, 1994), 7–8, 13.
4. Jer 29:11 NASB.
5. William Ferris, *You Live and Learn, Then You Die and Forget It All!* (New York: Doublday, 1992).
6. The details of my learning about my son's homosexuality are shared in my other books, including chapter 3 of *Stick a Geranium in Your Hat and Be Happy!*
7. Thanks to freelance writer Sherrie Weaver, Denver, Colorado, for sharing this witticism.
8. My stuggles before finally coming to say "Whatever Lord!" and the relief I felt when I finally reached that point are described in chapter 3 of *Splashes of Joy in the Cesspools of Life* (Dallas: Word, 1992). Like this letter-writer, hundreds of people have told me that relinquishing their children to God—saying, "Whatever Lord!"—has been the turning point in their recovery.
9. James Russell Lowell, quoted in *Reader's Digest*, April 1995.
10. H. Jackson Brown, *Live and Learn and Pass It On*, vol. 3, quoted in *Reader's Digest*, June 1995.
11. Magnetic Graffiti Company.
12. From *The Exchange*, January-February-March 1994, 4.
13. Alice Steinback in the *Baltimore Sun*, quoted in *Reader's Digest*, November 1993.

14. Submitted by a friend of Spatula Ministries.
15. Magnetic Graffiti.
16. Ps. 89:15.

**Chapter 5.   Answers We Didn't Wanna Hear to Questions
                 We Didn't Wanna Ask**
 1. For details of Bill's accident, see chapter 2 of *Stick a Geranium
     in Your Hat and Be Happy.*
 2. Thanks to freelance writer Sherrie Weaver, Denver, Colorado,
     for sharing these witticisms.
 3. James 1:2–3.
 4. Billy Graham, quoted in the *Tampa Tribune,* 24 April 1995.
 5. Matt. 11:28.
 6. See John 11:33–35.
 7. Jer. 29:11.
 8. Isa. 43:2.
 9. See Daniel 3.
10. Ps. 30:1–5, 11.
11. Phil. 4:13 NKJV.
12. Ps. 121:2.
13. James Dobson, *Life on the Edge* (Dallas: Word, 1995).
14. Prov. 25:2.
15. Deut. 29:29 NKJV.
16. Eccles. 11:5.
17. Isa. 55:8–9.
18. Norma Barzman, "Best Years," *Los Angeles Herald Examiner,* 6
     September 1989.
19. Henry Ward Beecher, cited in Wooten, *Heart, Humor, and
     Healing,* 1.
20. Prov. 17:22 TEV.
21. Prov. 15:15 TLB, adapted.
22. Adapted from *Laughing Matters,* edited by Joel Goodman,
     vol. 9, no. 2, 1993.
23. Adapted from *Reader's Digest,* April 1995, 86.
24. From Judy Garnatz Harriman's "Action" column in the *St.
     Petersburg (Fla.) Times,* 2 April 1995. Copyright 1995, *St.
     Petersburg Times.* Some items contributed by other news-
     papers. Used by permission.
25. Phillips, *Encyclopedia of Good Clean Jokes,* 183.
26. Rovin, *1001 Great One Liners,* 78.

27. Ibid., 27.
28. Virginia Satir, quoted in Jack Canfield and Mark Victor Hansen, *Chicken Soup for the Soul* (Deerfield Beach, Fla.: Health Communications, 1993).
29. Eccles. 3:1, 4 TLB.

Chapter 6.   All Stressed Up and No Place to Go!
1. Jane McAlister Pope, *Charlotte Observer*, reprinted in the *Tampa Tribune*, 5 August 1995.
2. Helen Lowrie Marshall, "Answered Prayer," *Quiet Power* (Grand Rapids: Baker, n.d.; distributed by Marshall Enterprises). Used by permission of copyright-holder Warren Marshall, Marshall Enterprises, Littleton, Colorado.
3. Charles Swindoll, *Strengthening Your Grip* (Dallas: Word, 1990).
4. *Good Housekeeping*, September 1995, 82.
5. Ibid.
6. Dietitian Susan Mitchell, quoted in the *Tampa Tribune*, 23 February 1995.
7. Rev. 1:7 KJV.
8. "'Twas the Night Before Jesus Came," © 1985 Bethany Farms, Inc. Used by permission of Jeffrey Cummings, Bethany Farms, Inc., St. Charles, Missouri.
9. Rovin, *1001 Great One-Liners*, 134.
10. Prov. 12:25 TLB.
11. Pat Hansen, 1994 Patprints Calendar.
12. 2 Tim. 1:7 NKJV.

Chapter 7.   You Are the Answer to Several Problems I Didn't Even Know I Had Until I Met You
1. Prov. 11:25.
2. Ps. 84:5–6 TLB.
3. Hunter Adams, M.D., quoted in Meladee McCarty and Hanock McCarty, *Acts of Kindness: How to Create a Kindness Revolution* (Deerfield Beach, Fla.: Health Communications, 1994).
4. Job 22:30 AMP.
5. E. C. McKenzie, *14,000 Quips and Quotes for Writers and Speakers* (New York: Greenwich House, n.d.).
6. Vera Robinson, R.N., Ed.D., in Patty Wooten, *Heart, Humor, and Healing*, 70.

7. Reprinted from a greeting card published by Portal Publications, San Francisco. Used by permission of Anthony Westling.

8. Brown, *Live and Learn and Pass It On*, vol. 3.

9. See this story in John 5:2–15. Jesus' question is in verse 6; emphasis is mine.

10. McKenzie, *14,000 Quips and Quotes for Writers & Speakers.*

11. Reprinted by permission of the publishers and Trustees of Amherst College from *The Poems of Emily Dickinson*, Thomas H. Johnson, ed., Cambridge, Mass.: The Belknap Press of Harvard University Press, copyright © 1951, 1955, 1979, 1983 by the president and fellows of Harvard College.

12. Mark Twain in *Pudd'nhead Wilson*, quoted in *The New International Dictionary of Quotations*, Hugh Rawson and Margaret Miner, comp. (New York: New American Library-Signet, 1986).

13. This poem by the late Pearl "Mama" Waddell is used with permission from her great-granddaughter, Shirley G. Boozer.

14. The Rev. Thomas J. Thompson, a member of the Health/AIDS Subcommittee of the Presbytery of Tampa Bay, Florida, quoted by columnist Mike Wilson in the *St. Petersburg Times*, 22 April 1995.

15. Dave Barry, *Stay Fit and Healthy Until You're Dead*, ed. Roger Yepsen (Emmaus, Pa.: Rodale, 1985).

16. Gal. 6:9–10.

Chapter 8.   I'd Like to Live Life in the Fast Lane, But I'm Married to a Speed Bump!

1. Matt. 12:34 KJV.

2. Adapted from Richard R. Rubin, Ph.D., June Biermann, and Barbara Toohey, *Psyching Out Diabetes, A Positive Approach to Your Negative Emotions* (Los Angeles: Lowell House, 1993). Reprinted with permission of RGA Publishing Group, Inc.

3. Virginia Valentine, RN, June Biermann, and Barbara Toohey, *Diabetes Type II and What to Do* (Los Angeles: Lowell House, 1993). Reprinted with permission of RGA Publishing Group, Inc.

4. "Fifty Famous Parental Sayings" by comedian Andy Andrews, author of the bestselling book *Storms of Perfection*. Used with permission of Robert D. Smith, First Image.

5. *Old Age Is Not for Sissies*, Lois Kaufman, comp. (White Plains, N.Y.: Peter Pauper Press, 1989).
6. Heb 12:12 TLB.
7. James 1:2.
8. Isa. 41:10.
9. Tom Wilson, Universal Press Syndicate, quoted in *Reader's Digest*, April 1995.
10. "Words of Wisdom from Mr. Hooty," *Pryor (Okla.) Herald.*
11. Adapted from idea 24: "Write It Down," in Stephen Arterburn and Carl Dreizler, *52 Simple Ways to Say "I Love You"* (Nashville: Oliver Nelson, 1991), 70.
12. Maxine 1995 Calendar, Shoebox Greetings, a division of Hallmark Cards, Inc.
13. *Good Housekeeping*, January 1996, 126.
14. Rovin, *1001 Great One-Liners.*
15. Duck Edwing, "Tribute Toon," *Tampa Tribune*, 15 September 1995.
16. Prov. 28:13 TLB.

Chapter 9. No, Peggy Lee, That's NOT All There Is!

1. From "Buried Alive" © 1978 by Rich Cook. Used by permission.
2. Ps. 90:10 KJV.
3. Mabel Camp (1871–1937), "He Is Coming Again"© 1913; renewed 1941 by N. H. Camp. Alfred B. Smith, owner.
4. See Eccles. 12:3–7.
5. See Rev. 21:4.
6. Adapted from the *Kleinknecht Encyclopedia.*
7. The author of this beautiful poem, "Think," is unknown. I found it on a card published by Missionary Servants of the Most Holy Trinity, Trinity Missions, Silver Spring, Maryland 20907.

Other Books by Barbara Johnson from Word

Stick a Geranium in Your Hat and Be Happy!

Splashes of Joy in the Cesspools of Life

Pack Up Your Gloomees in a Great Big Box

Mama, Get the Hammer!